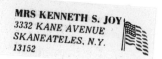

FIRST PRESBYTERIAN CHURCH
SKANEATELES, NEW YORK

#17

D1566836

#17

PERRY MARGARET
THE NEW CHRISTMAS MAGIC

THE NEW
CHRISTMAS MAGIC

THE ART OF MAKING
DECORATIONS & ORNAMENTS

THE NEW
CHRISTMAS MAGIC

THE ART OF MAKING
DECORATIONS & ORNAMENTS

☆ ☆ ☆

Revised edition of the book first published
under the title *Christmas Magic*

Margaret Perry

PHOTOGRAPHS AND DRAWINGS BY THE AUTHOR

DOUBLEDAY & COMPANY, INC., GARDEN CITY, NEW YORK

ACKNOWLEDGMENTS

To my family and friends for their interest and inspiration, and to Sigrid and Dolf Swing, for letting me photograph in their Connecticut country home, I give my sincere thanks.

ISBN: 0-385-05228-6
Library of Congress Catalog Card Number 75–5265
Copyright © 1964, 1975 by Margaret Perry
All Rights Reserved
Printed in the United States of America

CONTENTS

LIST OF COLOR ILLUSTRATIONS

INTRODUCTION

Christmas is a magic time, a time for reverie and reverence, fun and frolic, a time to look forward to and a time to look back upon. Christmas is a magic time all around the world.

Each corner of the globe has its own way of celebrating the holidays. And every city round the world, like a star in the earth's crown, sparkles in its own way, a little special in its traditions, its kinds of decorations, its tributes to the holiday season. Every family, in turn, has its own way of expressing the holiday mood—its particular preferences for decorating the Christmas tree, the wreath, the fireside.

To make Christmas really your own, you must create in your own special way. The symbols are universal—the tree, angels, candles, wreaths, stars, bells. Your own interpretations of these traditional symbols of the holiday season give a distinction to your celebration of Christmas.

Start with one idea, perhaps one you've seen or been told about, and before the idea is completed it will be a little different, a little individual, just a bit more personal—your own way of doing it. And as you go along, one idea will lead to another, until you'll find there are so many lovely things to do and make you won't know where to begin and where to stop.

Before you begin your decorations, decide upon an over-all plan, a particular color scheme, a theme to which variations can be added, so that there will be a continuity to your accomplishments. Choose, as the Chinese do, a motif for the year—make it, perhaps, the year of the angel, or the year of the star—and decide ahead of time what colors you'd especially like to have. The year of the angel might be gold and silver, for instance, and the year of the tiny trees green and blue. Don't limit your decorations to the single motif, but make it dominant.

Tradition is the foundation of the Christmas holiday season. We all have our special collection of treasures that make up a part of the tradition for us— the crimson Santa, the golden star that has always hung just *so* on the tree. Each year these treasures are carefully packed away when the holiday is over, to be taken out of their wrappings, with fond thoughts and many memories, when the season comes round again. Add some of your creations to your collection of treasures. Start your own "traditions" and add to them as the years go by.

Christmas never comes quickly enough when we are young. Remember how we used to say, "Wait a minute, I'm coming," and the impatient playmate would call, "So is Christmas!" But as we grow older Christmas comes all too quickly and often catches us unawares. If we make December the holiday month, as our Scandinavian friends do, and begin our preparations early, we'll be ready for the festive days that start with Christmas Eve.

PREFACE TO THIS REVISED EDITION

Since *Christmas Magic* first came out, there have been several new materials available for crafts—new kinds of glue and paste, such as Pritt Glue Stick, in unusual and easy-to-use containers, new varieties of paper in a wealth of textures and colors, better forms of materials for stuffing and padding, such as Poly-fil—which is pure polyester fiber—plastics in many shapes and forms, new tapes and trimmings and cords and laces—an abundance such as one could never find before.

Not only have materials changed, but our concepts of decorating have taken different directions, expanding and developing year by year. Today much more thought and importance is given to handcrafted objects. We are aware as never before of the need for conserving our resources, for re-using materials that come to us in the form of packaging and wrappings, as greeting cards and other so-called expendables.

With these changes in mind, we have revised and expanded *Christmas Magic*. We have added sections to existing chapters, removed some chapters entirely, and added others. We have included a chapter on how to make dolls for the Christmas scene much as our ancestors did, using scraps from the family patch-box and materials readily at hand in the kitchen. But today we can produce these handcrafted dolls with greater ease, with modern glues and materials readily available to us. We have added another chapter on how to make our own Christmas cards. With so much valuable material at hand, we find that handcrafting our own cards is one of the great pleasures of the season.

By keeping the best of the old and adding much that is new, we hope the *New Christmas Magic* will provide many hours of pleasure in the making of magic for Christmas.

THE NEW
CHRISTMAS MAGIC

THE ART OF MAKING
DECORATIONS & ORNAMENTS

☆

CHAPTER I

DOLLS FOR THE CHRISTMAS SCENE

As long as there are children—young or old—there will be dolls at Christmastime. In the days of long ago, dolls were made at home from whatever materials were at hand. Heads were carved from apples, eggs and nuts were given faces, and cornhusks were used for the complete figure.

With such materials collected in the fields and a few scraps of calico found in the family patchbox—and just a touch of magic in the making—you can create dolls that take on personalities all their own as they begin to come to life and take their places in the family scene.

EGG-HEAD DOLL

First, blow out the contents of the egg. To do this, make a small hole in each end with a sharp needle or the point of a small pair of scissors. Blow in one end and the contents will come out the other. The large end of the egg will be the top of the doll's head.

Next, give the head a hairdo. If you want your doll to have braids, glue 10-inch pieces of yarn across the top of the head and down the back, as shown in the photograph. Separate into halves and then braid each half. Tie with ribbon.

If you like, you can leave the hair unbraided and give it bangs across the front. If you use heavy yarn, each strand will look like a curl.

For the body, make a cone of cardboard about 7 inches tall, using one-quarter of a circle 14 inches in diameter. Secure with masking tape or glue. Snip off the top ½ inch of the cone so the egg head will fit nicely at the neck.

About ½ inch down from the neck (and before you put on the head), make a small hole on each side for the arms. Run a 12-inch pipe cleaner through these two holes, and secure at shoulders with masking tape. Make loops at ends for hands, and wrap the arms with a small amount of Poly-fil to give them form. You can also use cotton batting for this. Pad the chest too.

Glue the head to the body with Elmer's Glue, and let the glue set until it is quite dry. If you use one of the white glues, such as Elmer's or Sobo, it will take no more than eight or ten minutes to set, and then the head will be securely fastened.

1

How to Make No-Sew Doll Clothes

With the new stick glues readily available, the making of doll's clothes has become a matter of moments, instead of hours of needlework. You can now put the seams together with one or two sweeps of the glue stick along the seam to be fastened. In no time at all the doll can be dressed.

For the egg-head doll, start with the sleeves. Cut straight pieces of calico or gingham about 5 inches long and 2 inches wide. (See diagram.) Glue the hem (at the wrist) and the long seam together with Pritt Glue Stick, slip the sleeve over the padded arm, and secure to the top of the shoulder with masking tape. Tie at the wrists with ribbon or yarn.

Next comes the bodice. For this use a straight piece of fabric about 4 inches wide and 6 inches long. Make a small round hole for the neck and cut the bodice down the back (see diagram). Turn in the sides, secure with Pritt Glue Stick, and put the bodice on the doll. Glue the back seam together. The bodice should cover the tops of the sleeves.

For the skirt, use a straight piece of material and make the skirt as full as you like—more fullness for the little-girl doll, less for a lady doll (see the photographs).

Glue the hem and back seam, and glue the skirt over the bodice to the doll's waist, gathering it as you glue. Finish with a sash.

For a bonnet, use a half circle, about 2¼ inches in diameter, cut out of cardboard. Cover it with fabric to match the dress. A full circle will cover both sides of the bonnet. Turn in the rounded edges and fasten them together with glue. Decorate with ribbons, also attached with glue.

Tie or glue the bonnet to the doll's head.

The last thing to do—the very last!—is to draw the face. The surface of an egg is smudge-prone, so do this last.

I use a fine-pointed brown felt pen for

the eyebrows, eyes, and nose (which is only two tiny dots), and a red felt pen to draw the mouth. Give the cheeks a touch of rouge.

THE WALNUT-HEAD DOLL

This is made exactly like the egg-head doll, except that the cone should be about an inch shorter to accommodate the smaller head.

The seam of the walnut shell makes the nose. And since the walnut gives the appearance of a very wrinkled face, the walnut-head doll is usually a little old lady. Use white yarn for the hair. Start at the center of the back of the head (which will be on the seam) and spiral the hair into a fashionable lady's hairdo. Use white glue to attach the yarn.

Make the costume in the same way as for the egg-head doll, but, since this will be an old-lady doll, use less material in the skirt.

For an umbrella, cut a third of a circle of bright colored construction pa-

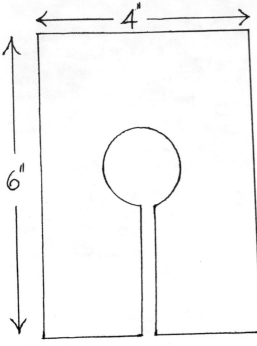

per about 6 inches in diameter. Fold in accordion-pleat fashion. When it is folded together, snip the tops to make them rounded. Glue the paper umbrella to a pipe-cleaner handle, turning over the top of the handle for a crook to hang on the lady's arm.

For a basket, use a half walnut shell. Glue a piece of pipe cleaner to each side (inside) for a basket handle. Stuff the "basket" with a piece of bright fabric.

There are many variations that can be made. The egg-head doll can have a large hair bow and long dark hair, or

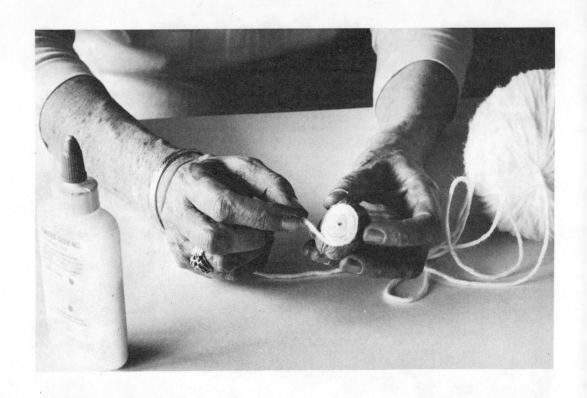

she can have a bun at the back of the neck; the walnut-head doll can have a gingham skirt and a red shawl, with a red baboushka on her head. Her broom can be made with a few sprigs of dried weed glued to a dried flower stem.

Stand your dolls under the Christmas tree. They will brighten the scene and delight all the "children" in the family.

CORNHUSK DOLLS

This is an old-fashioned craft that is finding new popularity in many parts of the world today. These dolls have been made for hundreds of years, both here and abroad, and although the theory is that the Indians taught the American colonists how to make them, some records seem to indicate that they were made in Europe as well as America, and many years ago.

If you plan to make dolls out of your cornhusks, take the husks carefully off the cob, spread them out on a newspaper, and let them dry completely. Place a second newspaper on top of the husks, smoothing them out carefully, so they will dry quite flat. This takes about a week.

When you are ready to make your doll, soak the dried husks for a few minutes in warm water—just long enough to make them workable.

For the head, tear off a strip of husk about ½ inch wide and roll it into a ball. Add strips until you have a ball large

enough for the head—about an inch across. Secure with a drop of glue or a straight pin.

Next, tear off narrow strips and wind them around a 12-inch-long pipe cleaner for the arms. Secure the ends of the strips with a dot of glue, and tie at the wrists with string or thread—or a narrow strip of husk.

For the body, roll strips of husk into a ball as for the head, but make the ball a little larger. Then, find a long (as long as possible), smooth piece of husk, about an inch wide, and drape it over the head. Tie under the chin with heavy thread or string; put the arms under the chin (inside the long piece of husk) and tie once more. Slip the body up under the arms, and tie once more—this will be the doll's waist.

Half-inch-wide strips, crisscrossed over the shoulders, make the doll's blouse. Fasten the ends with glue.

The skirt is made with many wide strips of husk. Place them around the waist, pointed end up, layer upon layer, until you have a full skirt. Tie with string or heavy thread, and finish with a sash of husk.

The skirt must be trimmed straight across the bottom because this is what the doll stands on.

If you would like to give your doll a bouffant skirt, fasten extra husks to her waist, but put them on upside down. (See photograph.) Tie them tightly, and then drop them down to form an unusually attractive, bustlelike, 1890 style of skirt.

Cornhusks take dyes easily. You can use cold-water dyes or regular food coloring. Dye the husks before you start to work with them to make your doll.

9

☆

CHAPTER II

THE CHRISTMAS VILLAGE

When you are planning your Christmas decorations, you will want to include a Christmas village to symbolize peace and good will, a tranquil setting in a wintry landscape inhabited by many kinds of creatures.

The Christmas village sometimes settles under the Christmas tree, sometimes on the mantel. One year it appeared on the wide window sill of my living-room casement window.

My village always contains the treasures I've collected from other lands— the little wooden figure of the Norwegian girl with a long trumpet calling her herd of goats; the colorful Swedish horses that are now so popular; the horses' cousin, the zebra, made of wood with a grain that looks like stripes; the French rooster; the Russian doll; the Chinese dancer; the three little elves and the little straw lamb from Denmark. And mixed in with these are several creatures I've made.

Buildings for the village are made of Bristol board or construction paper in various colors, with doors and windows of small pieces of colored cellophane tape.

The village can be set up on white cotton batting, and if you'd like a lake in your snowy scene, set a piece of unframed mirror on the cotton.

VILLAGE CHURCH

The focal point of the village is, of course, the church. This one is made of white Bristol board, trimmed with red and green cellophane tape.

The steeple is made from an 8-inch by 7-inch piece of board, cut according to the diagram. Fold on dotted lines and glue together, tucking in tab to form a four-sided steeple. The points of the steeple are held together with strips of colored cellophane tape—I used green along the points (the roof) and then I covered the corners of the four walls with red tape, to give definition to the little structure. The door is made of one green strip and one red strip of cellophane tape, tapered at the top.

For the main part of the church, start with a piece of board 12 inches long and 3¾ inches wide. Cut according to the diagram, and fold along the dotted lines. Glue together, tucking tab inside one wall.

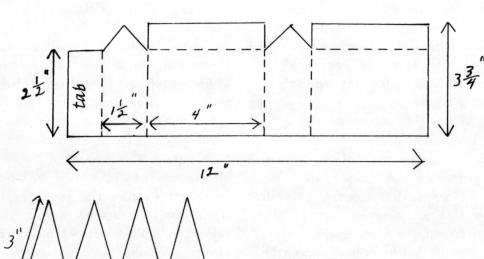

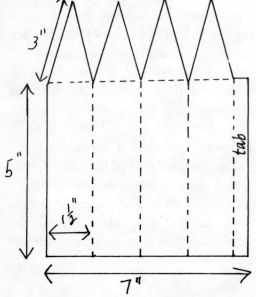

The roof is held together with cellophane tape and the corners and eaves are outlined with tape. The windows are small pieces of cellophane tape, pointed to match the door.

You can, if you like, attach the steeple to the church. I leave mine separate because it is easier to store away.

THE ROOSTER

The rooster is made in bright colors. Use construction paper, Bristol board, or metallic foil. I used construction paper for mine.

Start with a Circle

Cut a circle 6 inches in diameter. Using only about one third of the circle, staple together to form a cone. Snip off the point of the cone ½ inch down.

Cut out the head, following the pattern given here. Fit the long tab into the cone and fasten with a touch of Sobo glue.

For the rooster's tail, cut two strips, each ½ inch wide: one strip 4 inches long and the other 3½ inches long. Make them of different colors. Fringe the ends, curl them around a pencil, and glue or staple them to the base of the cone so they will stand up as shown in the photograph.

Good colors to use for the rooster: yellow for the body, red for the head and lower tail, green for the upper tail; blue for the body, yellow for the head and lower tail, red for the upper tail. Whatever colors you use, mix them up and make them bright, for the rooster should be perky.

VILLAGE BARN

The village barn and silo are made of red construction paper. Let the children make this one—it's simple to put together and the pieces are easy to cut.

For the barn cut a piece of paper 18 inches long and 4 inches wide. Cut according to the diagram, using the measurements given. Fold along the dotted lines indicated in the sketch and glue together, tucking the tab inside one wall. This will give you a barn 6 inches long, 2½ inches wide, and 4 inches high.

For the roof, cut a piece of paper 5½ inches by 6½ inches, which will allow for a bit of overhang, and fold on dotted lines as indicated in the diagram. Fasten it to the barn with a few spots of glue.

The silo stands beside the barn—it is not attached to it. Cut a strip 9 inches long and 6 inches wide. Staple the short edges together to form the tower. For the silo roof, cut a 5-inch circle, make a slit from one edge to the center, and then overlap the two resulting edges until you have the desired cone shape—you will use about three quarters of the circle. Staple together and glue to the silo tower.

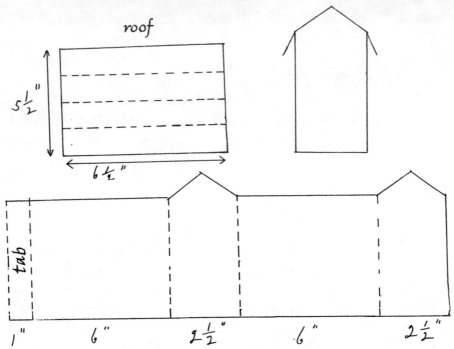

roof

$5\frac{1}{2}"$

$6\frac{1}{2}"$

tab

$1"$ $6"$ $2\frac{1}{2}"$ $6"$ $2\frac{1}{2}"$

THE MOUSE

One of the most ingratiating creatures in my Christmas village is the little white mouse. He is made of plain white paper—regular bond typing paper is excellent.

Start with a Circle

Out of plain white paper cut a circle 6 inches in diameter. Using only about one third of the circle, as indicated in the diagram shown here, form a cone, stapling it more than an inch down from the edge of the cone.

With a small pair of scissors, cut away about an inch of the cone on the stapled side (see diagram), tapering the cone smoothly so the mouse will sit down.

A 6-inch strip of paper, ¼ inch wide, is curled up (use a pencil for this) and attached with cellophane tape or a bit of glue for his tail. Attach large, rounded ears with a bit of glue, and make tiny black eyes with pen and ink. And presto! Your mouse is completed.

I always make several of these—one for the village, one for the cheese tray, and several to scamper among the branches of the Christmas tree.

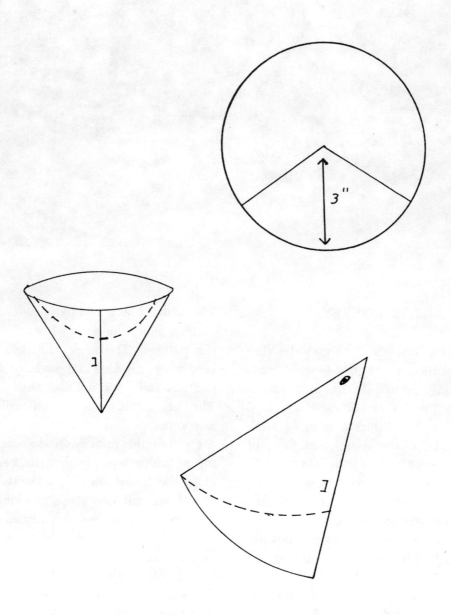

3"

1

1

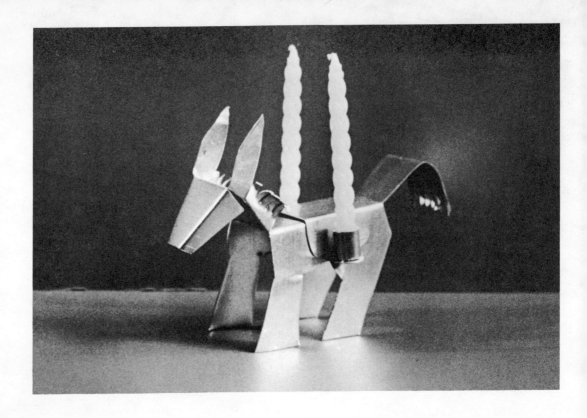

THE DONKEY

Carrying candles on his saddle, the donkey brings a soft glow to the Christmas village scene. He stands 4 inches high—to the tip of his ears—and is 6 inches long from his nose to his tail. He's made of aluminum, and thus, of course, is kept from year to year.

Trace the pattern given here onto the aluminum with a pencil. Ordinary household scissors will cut the aluminum quite easily—it always reminds me of cutting through cheese. Cutting the donkey accurately takes a bit of patience and care, but he's fetching and he's sturdy, and he lasts from year to year.

Smooth the rough edges with sandpaper or an emery board, and polish very gently with the finest steel wool.

This makes him gleam like pewter.

Bend along the dotted lines shown in the pattern: The neck, the mane, the ears go up; his face and jowls go down; and his tail goes up and then down. The curls in his mane and tail will form as you cut.

Cut out the donkey's saddle according to the pattern given, again bending along the dotted lines. To make the candleholders, cut two strips of aluminum ½ inch by 1⅝ inches. Bend around the base of a 3½-inch candle to get the proper size, and attach to the saddle with liquid solder. Let the solder dry thoroughly—several hours—before putting candles into the holders. Use the non-drip kind.

Paint the saddle a bright color, or polish it with steel wool for a silvery shine.

[1] The Christmas village is assembled under the Christmas tree on a snowy landscape of cotton. Poly-fil works well too. See Chapter II.

[2] Wall sconce of aluminum made in the shape of a Christmas tree shines like pewter in the candlelight. Chapter V.

[3] To hang on the wall or stand on a table, aluminum sconce can be made in many different shapes, including the fleur-de-lis. For instructions, see Chapter V.

[4] Bell pull for the door is made of red felt and trimmed with sleigh bells and gold braid. Instructions in Chapter III.

[5] The apple pyramid, a traditional English Christmas decoration, was popular in early America. See Chapter IV.

[6] The copper angel holds her candles to light up the Swedish *rosmåling* plate. Instructions for making the angel are in Chapter V.

[7] Angel ring trimmed with strands of princess pine hangs over the party buffet table. Instructions are given in Chapter VII.

8] Shadow boxes can be made with Christmas cards as backgrounds, to feature figurines or other treasures. See Chapter IX.

[9] A big red bow and a cluster of foil bells decorate a doorway. Directions for making the bells are given in Chapter III.

[10] A mobile made of five paper birds in contrasting colors is made on copper wire. For instructions, see Chapter VIII.

[11] A green felt mat, trimmed with golden braid and sequins, protects the coffee table. Instructions in Chapter IV.

[13] A candle on a liqueur glass brightens the cookie tray. See Chapter V.

[12] Goblets are turned into candlesticks, with bright Christmas balls inside. See Chapter V.

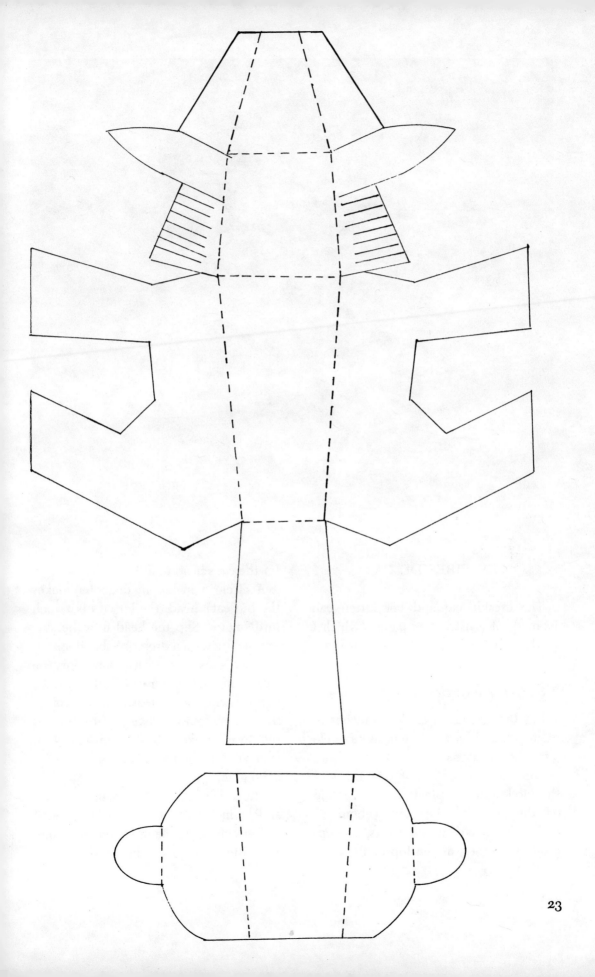

23

THE FIRESIDE CAT

The fireside cat and her kitten can be made of construction paper (which I used), metallic foil, or Bristol board.

Start with a Circle

For the cat, cut a circle 10 inches in diameter; and for the kitten, use a circle 5 inches in diameter.

Form a cone of about one third of the circle, and staple it together. Snip off the point of the cone (about ⅛ inch), and make two tiny slits, one opposite the other, at the top of the cone for the cat's head to fit into.

A circle 2 inches in diameter makes the big cat's head; the kitten's is 1 inch in diameter. Slip the head into the slits and secure with a drop of Sobo glue.

Make ears 1½ inches long for the cat, 1 inch long for the kitten. Make them pointed and crease them through the center, folding them slightly toward the face. Make whiskers of sprigs of evergreen or of paper, and attach with Sobo glue.

The tail of the cat is 6 inches long and ½ inch wide. Curl it over a pencil and attach with glue or cellophane tape. The kitten's tail is 4 inches long.

THE THREE WISE MEN

The Three Wise Men, in their royal garb, are a part of every Christmas scene. Make them of colorful paper or foil, and choose your colors with care. My kings are blue and purple and red —all royal colors. The blue one has a crown and cope of green; the purple one has a pink crown and cope; and the red one has gold.

Start with a Circle

Make a cone of one quarter of a 9-inch circle—this will give you a slender cone. Cut the cope according to the pattern given. Fasten it around the shoulders of the king with a spot of glue, overlapping the points until they form a smooth, curved line for the cope from front to back.

Cut the crown from the pattern given (same color for the crown and cope) and form a ring by overlapping the two points and securing with glue. Slip the crown over the point of the cone. Fasten with a dab of glue.

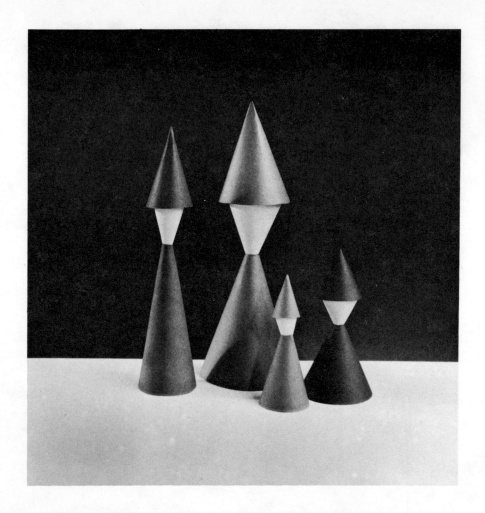

THE *TOMTE*

In Scandinavia the Christmas elf is called a *tomte* (tom'-tah). Tomtes are almost always red and are made of paper, wood, yarn, foil, and even of straw, and are used to decorate everything from Christmas trees to packages. And usually there are tomtes on the Christmas dinner table.

Here is a modern version of the Christmas tomte. These are made of construction paper—red for the body and cap, and white for the head—and they can be tall or short, fat or slim.

Start with a Circle

The tall tomte in the center of the photograph is about 10 inches high. Cut a circle of red construction paper 10 inches in diameter. Using only about one third of the circle, form a cone and staple or glue it together. Snip off about ½ inch of the point of the cone.

Next, cut a circle of white construction paper 5½ inches in diameter. Again using only one third of the circle, form a cone and fasten it with staples or glue.

Dip a toothpick into Sobo glue, run it around the inside of the "neck" of the

red cone, and insert the pointed end of the white cone, thus fastening the head to the body.

The third cone—which will be the cap—is made of a circle 7 inches in diameter, cut from red construction paper. Once more, using only one third of the circle, form a cone and fasten it together with glue or staples.

Again dip the toothpick in the glue, and this time run it around the outside edge of the top of the white cone, and set the cap on the head. In a few moments the glue will dry—and your tomte will be finished.

For a slimmer elf, use less than a third of the circle for each of the three cones. And if you'd like him to be fatter, use about half of the circle. This, of course, will also make him shorter.

These little creatures add color and charm to the Christmas Eve buffet, the mantel, or along the stairway as shown here.

☆

CHAPTER III

BOWS AND BELLS FOR YOUR DOORS AND HALLS

Christmas Eve—the magic hour has come, and the world is full of carolers and candles. Warm welcomes wait at every door, and every door is decorated.

Your doorway gives a greeting to your guests and sends a warm glow out upon the winter landscape. The decorations you choose should reflect the mood of the household, be it modern and bright or completely traditional. Colors in themselves can reflect the modern mood—chartreuse, pale blue, crimson. Red and green with gold or silver, regardless of the design, give the traditional touch.

If your doorway is protected from the weather, you can choose from many materials the ones that suit you best. If wind and rain and snow and sleet will beat upon your windowpane, use plant materials and plastic ribbon for your outside decorations.

Inside doors can be decorated too. And the children of the family love their own doorway décor, especially if they make it themselves. Hall doors and kitchen doors, doors throughout the house—each can be decorated to reflect the décor found within.

RINGS OF HOLLY

To hang in a doorway or a hallway, here are three rings of holly tied with red velvet tubing—that ribbonlike strand of velvet that comes by the yard and is available in most five-and-ten-cent stores.

If you have holly bushes in your own garden, snip off about three dozen pieces 3 or 4 inches long. This pruning will not hurt the bushes—in fact, it will be good for next year's growth. If you don't have your own holly, you can find it at your local florist shop, or you can use artificial holly if you like.

Start with three sets of embroidery hoops, 7½ inches, 6 inches, and 5 inches in diameter. Open up each set to form a sphere, and wind very fine wire at the joints to keep the hoops in this position.

Tie a 3-yard length of red velvet tubing (or ribbon) to the top of the largest sphere, run it down through the center of the hoops and tie it to the bottom of the sphere. Then, leaving about 4 inches between, tie the ribbon to the next sphere in the same fashion, running it down through the circles and tying it at the bottom. Finally, again leaving

about 4 inches between, secure the smallest sphere.

Leave enough ribbon at the top to hang the rings by, and loop the end of the ribbon to finish off the bottom.

With very fine wire (it comes on a spool in ten-cent and hardware stores), attach the sprigs of holly to the hoops. It's a prickly job, but don't let that deter you. The results are lovely and well worth every prick.

SEED-POD WREATH

For a change from the usual evergreen wreath, one made of dried plant materials is colorful and interesting. Many different kinds of materials can be used: rose hips, acorn caps, teasel pods, astilbe blossoms, snowberries (some will dry white, some dark), coneflower pods, burdock, day-lily pods, and beechnut pods. The assortment gives the wreath its charm.

As a base you can use a Styrofoam circle of whatever size you like. Or you can cut a circle of heavy cardboard or corrugated cardboard as a base. If you cover the base carefully and completely, the edges of the base will not show.

Attach the seed pods with white glue (Sobo or Elmer's), and mix the assortment as you go. The variation of color

and texture, shape and form, will create an unusual wreath. To preserve it, spray with a clear plastic.

Tie a red ribbon on the wreath, or leave it completely plain. Either way, it will decorate your doorway beautifully.

CRANBERRY WREATH

For an inside door, you can make a colorful wreath by stringing cranberries on a wire, bending the wire into a circle and attaching another wire to hang it by.

Tie a red or green velvet ribbon bow to the wreath at the point where the wires meet, and hang an angel or a Santa Claus or a bell—or any one of your special Christmas treasures—inside the wreath.

The cranberries should be lacquered (clear nail polish will do nicely) in order to preserve them for the entire holiday season.

FUNNEL BELLS

Your kitchen door plays an important part in the holiday festivities. Through this doorway come all the goodies for the Christmas parties, the turkeys and hams, the fruits and vegetables, the finest food for family and friends that adds so much to the joy of the festive season.

There are many ways to decorate the kitchen door. These golden bells are made of ordinary kitchen funnels strung on golden cord.

Three 2½-inch funnels are covered with gold paint or spray. For the bottom bell I used a piece of gold cord about 16 inches long. I tied a small (1-inch)

Christmas ball in the center of the piece of cord, made a large knot about an inch above the ball so it would hang down inside the bell like a clapper, and then ran the double cord up through the funnel. I used about 14 inches of cord for the middle bell, and 12 inches for the top one, and made clappers of Christmas balls in each.

This cluster of bells is not only simple to make, it is quick as well, especially if you use a fast-drying gold paint. By the time you have finished painting the third bell, the first is ready to be fitted with a clapper.

Attach the bells to a branch of evergreens (I used long-needled pine) and hang the spray on the kitchen door.

METALLIC-FOIL BELLS

A cluster of bells tied to your doorway with evergreen branches will ring in the Christmas season.

Use metallic foil for these, and they will withstand the weather, at least for one season.

Start with a Circle

For every two bells, cut a circle 5 inches in diameter. Using half the circle, staple to form a cone, catching in the staple one end of a 15-inch piece of gold cord. Let the cord go through the point of the cone.

Make five or seven or as many bells as you like, and tie them together in a cluster. Attach them to sprays of evergreen with very fine wire, and hang on the door.

These bells are effective not only on a doorway but tied to the railing of your porch or outside stairway—or on a balcony railing, as shown here. Again you can mix the colors or make them all of gold or silver.

If you want the bells to predominate, be sparing of the greens. Choose an interestingly shaped branch of long-needled pine for an airy effect.

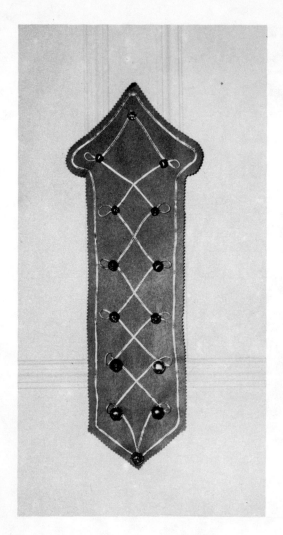

sträng you will need about 3 yards of gold braid and fourteen sleigh bells of different colors. Before cutting the felt, cut a pattern out of newspaper.

To make the pattern, fold a large sheet of newspaper in half. With a soft pencil, draw *half* of the design you have decided on, using the fold as the center line. Cut the pattern, open it up—and if the design doesn't suit you, try again!

When you have a design you like, place the pattern on the felt and cut with pinking scissors.

Attach gold braid to the felt either by sewing it on or by using glue. I prefer the glue because it is much quicker. Use Pritt Glue Stick—it works like a lipstick and does not smear.

Sew on sleigh bells at the points where the braid crosses, and sew on one at the center top and another at the center bottom.

Fasten the top of the klockasträng to your door with a thumbtack or brass-headed nail, leaving the bottom free so that your visitors can take hold of it to sound the bells on their arrival.

RED FELT *KLOCKASTRÄNG*

Made especially for your own door and made from your own design, a *klockasträng* has a great deal of charm. Here's one made of red felt, gold braid, and sleigh bells.

Start with a Strip

This strip is 23 inches long and 9 inches wide. To decorate the klocka-

TREASURE *KLOCKASTRÄNG*

Here is a klockasträng that has become a family tradition, a treasure that has grown with the years.

Start with a Strip

The strip is red felt, 20 inches long and 3 inches wide, cut out with pinking scissors. A dark-green inch-wide satin ribbon is sewn down through the middle of the red felt. On this ribbon are attached bells and buttons of particular significance—a bell from a daughter's favorite party costume, crystal buttons from a special dress, the square wooden buttons that brightened a wool jacket—each one bringing, year by year, another decoration to the doorpull.

Winding its way down among the baubles is a narrow gold cord, circling at the bottom a single, sizable sleigh bell that had been worn by the daughter on her shoe in Morris dances during her school days. The family initial—S— on an ivory button finishes the strand.

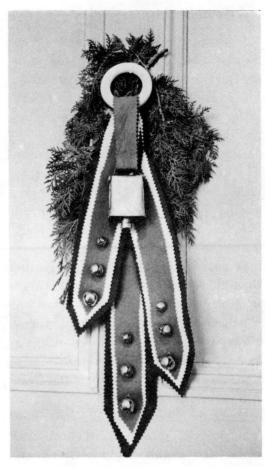

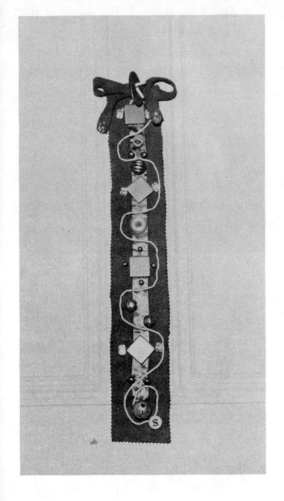

SLEIGH-BELL *KLOCKASTRÄNG*

In Scandinavia klockasträngs (bell pulls) are popular for doorway decorations at Christmas time. Traditionally, the klockasträng carried a cowbell—a bell that was available at every farm and village. Tied with ribbons and hung with greens, the bell was rung by visitors to announce their arrival. Today the cowbell is still used, and almost always it is painted gold.

The klockasträng shown here is made in the traditional style of strips of felt, sleigh bells, and a gold-painted cowbell.

Start with a Strip

Use green, red, and white felt—green for the background, white in the middle, and red on top. The green strips (there are three of each color) are 2½ inches wide, the white is 2 inches wide, and the red is 1½ inches wide.

Cut the strips with pinking scissors. The longest ones are 18, 17½, and 17 inches long; the middle ones 15, 14½, and 14 inches long; and the shortest ones are 12, 11½, and 11 inches long. Taper the ends to points.

Sew on sleigh bells right through the three thicknesses in a row, as I have, or in clusters.

Attach the three pulls to a ring—either wood, as here, or wire—using a heavy needle and strong thread. On a separate strip of red felt, hang the cowbell in the center.

Hang the klockasträng on your door with a spray of evergreens, and your friends and neighbors will let you know that they have arrived by ringing the cowbell. The sleigh bells will jingle too.

STAR OF GOLD

When Queen Anne's lace dries in the fall, it has an ethereal quality that can be captured for holiday decorations. A golden star to hang on your door or above the mantel is quick and easy to make.

The fragile-looking blossoms have a remarkable ruggedness. To make a star of these dried blossoms, start with a base of ordinary screening, cut in the shape of a five-pointed star about 12 inches in diameter.

First, make a pattern for your star (see Chapter VI for directions for making a five-pointed star), and then cut out the screening with a pair of kitchen scissors. Screening is available at all hardware stores.

Cover the star with dried blossoms of Queen Anne's lace, placing a large one in the center and in each point. Scatter the smaller blossoms among these. Leave about ¼ inch of stem on the blossoms, and insert these stems into the screen. You may have to enlarge the mesh with the point of your scissors to accommodate some of the thicker stems. Secure the stems with a dab of white glue. Spray the star with gold paint, attach a fine wire loop through the mesh at the back, and hang up your golden star.

For a jeweled look, glue a lacquered cranberry into the center of each blossom.

HOLLY BALL

A ball of holly that will keep fresh is made on a base of Oasis—the foamlike material that holds water.

Place a block of water-soaked Oasis in a pint-sized plastic strawberry basket, making a sort of cage by wiring on the bottom of a second basket for a cover.

Take a piece of wire about 4 inches long and loop it through the cage at the center of the top. To this loop tie a red velvet ribbon 1-inch wide and about a yard long. The holly ball will hang by this red velvet ribbon.

Insert sprigs of holly through the latticework of the basket into the Oasis until the container is completely hidden.

enlarge the hole with a pencil until you can run a velvet ribbon through the ball. Knot the ribbon at the top as well as at the bottom of the ball, insert sprigs of artificial holly (they will stay without glue), making sure the entire ball is covered. Suspend it by the ribbon.

A LACY GOLDEN BALL

Here's a golden ball to decorate a hall or a doorway.

Start with a Styrofoam ball 3 inches in diameter. Make a hole through the center of the ball, first using a wire and then a pencil to make it larger.

Run a moss-green velvet ribbon ½ inch wide and 1½ yards long through the hole, loop it twice at the bottom, and tuck the end up inside the ball. The long piece of ribbon at the top of the ball will serve to hang it by.

Next, cover the ball with dried Queen Anne's lace blossoms. Leave about ½ inch of stem on each blossom and stick the stems into the Styrofoam. Spray with gold. Wind tissue paper around the green ribbon to protect it while you are spraying.

Tie three or four red velvet bows to pieces of wire bent like hairpins, and insert these into the Oasis.

Hang the holly ball in a doorway or a hallway. Add a small amount of water each day to the center of the ball. Place a bowl or a newspaper underneath to catch the drops.

If you use artificial holly, use a Styrofoam ball as a base. Make a hole through the center of the ball with a wire, and

ORANGE-JUICE-CAN BELLS

The traditional Christmas colors—red, green, and gold—are used for this doorway swag, bringing brilliance and beauty to the back door.

The bells are made of frozen-orange-juice cans from which the tops have been completely removed. Cover the cans with gold paint (they'll probably need two coats), and punch a hole in the bottom of each can with a can opener or screw driver.

Run a wide (2 inches at least) red satin ribbon through each hole, knotting one end so that the can won't slip off. Tie the three bells together in such a way that each one hangs a little below the next, and attach to a big red bow and a bough of evergreens.

☆

CHAPTER IV

TABLES AND TREES

Nothing quite symbolizes Christmas for us as appropriately as does a tree. It is the focal point of festivities for most of us, the symbol of the season, especially for the children.

Table trees can be made in all shapes and sizes and of many different kinds of materials, from tiny trees of tissue paper to 2-foot-tall trees made of plant material. And in general, of course, the smallest table takes the littlest tree.

Tables take on significance, too, during the holiday season, for it is our tables that we decorate for all the Christmas parties—buffet tables, dining tables, hall tables, coffee tables, all kinds of tables large and small.

We all have our favorite ways of trimming our tables and trees. Here are some of mine.

APPLE PYRAMID

The traditional apple pyramid, sometimes called the Hospitality Pyramid, comes to us from England. It was a popular Christmas centerpiece during the eighteenth and nineteenth centuries. It can be used on the Christmas dinner table, on a mantel, or on a hall table. The fragrance of apples and evergreens signifies the season, giving an extra dimension to the treelike form. It is easy to make and will last for more than a week.

Start with a Styrofoam cone about 10 inches tall, thirteen regular-size apples, and about ten small apples. You will also need about 5 feet of ordinary iron wire of 14 gauge, and several sprays of evergreens. Shine up the apples before you begin the project.

In the bottom row of the pyramid there are seven apples. To attach the apples to the cone, cut seven pieces of wire, each about 4 inches long. Impale an apple on one end of each wire and insert the other end in the cone. Try to space the apples evenly, and remember that the spaces in between will be filled with evergreens. The second row from the bottom will take six apples. For the next three rows, use the smaller apples —five for the third row, four for the fourth, and one nice one for the very top of the cone. As the cone becomes narrower, shorten your pieces of wire.

When all the apples are in place, insert short sprigs of evergreens into the

Styrofoam cone to fill in the spaces between the apples. You can use balsam, hemlock, or any kind of pine. And if you have evergreens in your garden, prune them a little and use the cuttings for your pyramid.

Place the finished pyramid on a tray and decorate with a circle of evergreens.

SNOWBALL TREE

The snowball tree was made especially as the centerpiece for a children's party. Surrounded by snowman place cards and decorated with sprigs of evergreen, it makes a most appealing setting.

The base of the tree is a 10-inch Styrofoam cone (or make a cone of cardboard). Cotton balls—the kind that

44

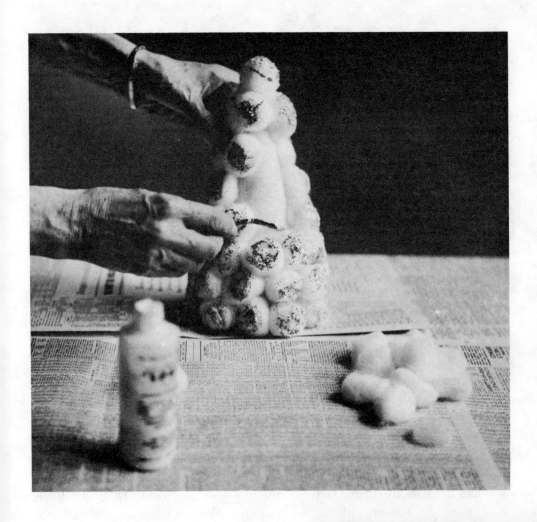

come packaged in cellophane for apply-
ing and removing cosmetics—make the
tree.

Dip each cotton ball in a bit of glue
and then in silver glitter, just one side
of the ball. Then, starting at the bottom
of the cone, glue the cotton balls in
place, putting the last one on the point
of the cone.

To add sparkle to the tree, glue tiny
silver Christmas balls (½ inch in diameter) into the spaces between the cotton
balls.

The finished tree is fluffy and snowy,
and it's icy-looking too.

SNOWMAN PLACE CARDS

The snowman is made by gluing two cotton balls together. Before gluing, compress the top one by rolling it between the palms of your hands, so that the snowman's head is a bit smaller than his body. Tie a piece of gold cord or colored ribbon around the neck.

For the hat, cut a circle of metallic foil (or colored construction paper) 1¼ inches in diameter. For the crown, cut a strip 1¼ inches by 2¼ inches, roll it up by gluing the short ends together, and attach to the center of the circle with glue. Another touch of glue will hold it to the snowman's head.

Attach the snowman, with glue, to a 2-inch by 3-inch card made of the same color and material as the hat.

Cut out of snapshots the face of each child invited to the party and paste each picture to a snowman. This, of course, requires the co-operation of all the mothers, but it is worth the effort just to watch the youngsters' glee when they find their faces on the snowmen.

Snowman place cards are fun for family parties too, for children and grownups alike.

GLITTER TREE

Trees covered with glitter add brightness to a table by reflecting the light from Christmas candles. Use them to trim a party table or in the Christmas village.

Start with a Circle

Make a cone of one third of a 10-inch circle of green construction paper, stapling it together. Cover the cone with Sobo glue and roll it in glitter that has been scattered on a newspaper.

Snip off the point of the cone (no more than ⅛ inch) and insert a small Christmas ball on a pipe cleaner. If you have used silver glitter, use a silver Christmas ball—gold glitter with a gold ball. Or use a green Christmas ball to match the green cone base, which will show through the glitter.

TREE OF DRIED BLOSSOMS

For table decorations, for favors at your Christmas party, for color in your Christmas village—tiny trees of dried blossoms have many uses.

Start with a Circle

Use construction paper or lightweight cardboard. A circle 7 inches in diameter will make three trees. Cut the circle into thirds and staple each third to form a cone.

Starting at the bottom of the cone, I carefully placed dried blossoms of red- and gold-colored strawflowers so that the colors would be mixed evenly, attaching the flowers with a touch of Sobo glue and topping the tree with one red blossom.

The whole process took me quite a

long time, and when the tree was finished a friend of mine, who had been watching me, looked askance at the clock. "I have five children coming home from school," she said, "and my husband will arrive on the six twenty-nine. Dinner guests are coming, and I need just such tiny trees for my table. But I haven't much time."

She cut a circle, made a cone with one third of it, smeared it with glue, and rolled it in the dried blossoms, which she had scattered on a newspaper. In no time she had her tree—you can judge for yourself from the photograph which one appeals to you. The "quickie" is on the left.

Three tiny tomtes from Denmark—they are made of wood and their caps are painted red, so that the colors blend well with the gold and red blossoms—give the tree dimension.

SEGMENTED PAPER TREE

When you make a tree for your
Christmas village, you can make it of
green construction paper—or if your
scene is snowy, you can make it of plain
white bond typing paper.

Start with a Square

For the green tree, cut four 6-inch
squares. For the white tree, cut twelve
squares. Both trees are made in the
same way, as follows:

Fold each square in half and cut according to the pattern given. When all
sections of the tree are cut, open each
one flat, stack them all up, and staple
three times along the crease made down
through the center of the "trunk"—staple at top and bottom and in the middle. Be as careful as you can to get the
staple right on the crease.

Open up the tree by gently folding
each leaf until the segments are evenly
spaced, and stand it up.

To keep your tree for another year,
fold it flat and store it away.

If you want to make a snowy scene
on a small table—perhaps in the hall or
on the coffee table—place two or three
cotton-ball snowmen beside the little
white tree.

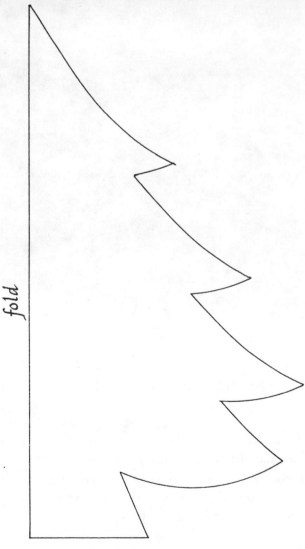

fold

KNITTING-NEEDLE TREE

The knitting-needle tree is a glamorous one that can be used for the hall table, the mantel, or as a centerpiece for the dining table. For this tree you can mix your colors or keep them within a color scheme.

Start with a knitting needle 14 inches long. Be sure it is the kind that has a metal cap at the blunt end to keep the stitches from falling off. String four large Christmas balls (each about 4 inches in diameter) onto the needle, slipping the little metal loops on the balls over the point of the needle. These four balls will form the base of the tree,

and if you place them squarely on a table, they will hold the needle upright.

Next, string onto the needle four balls of a slightly smaller size. Each one will fit between two of the larger ones. Then string on another four, slightly smaller, and finally four more, again slightly smaller, so that your tree has sixteen Christmas balls in all. On the top of the needle place a Christmas-tree peak.

If you want to move the tree, take off the peak and pick up the tree by the point of the knitting needle.

Experiment with your colors. Try a different color for each size—say, red, green, blue, and gold—or try four balls of varying sizes in each color. This can give you a spiral effect. Sometimes I make mine entirely of silver and combine it with silver candlesticks holding red candles.

Decorate the base of the tree with evergreens or holly or place it on a Christmas centerpiece made of felt, which you will find at the end of this chapter.

APPLE CENTERPIECE

Apples and evergreens from your own garden will make the perfect centerpiece for your holiday dinner table.

Remove the stems of eight lady apples —or crab apples—and scoop out holes large enough for 5-inch candles. If you want your centerpiece to last through the holidays, coat the apples with a clear lacquer to prevent shriveling.

String the apples on a piece of heavy wire (14-gauge) about 38 inches long, spacing the apples evenly. Bend wire into a circle and secure both ends in one apple. You could, of course, just stand the apples in a ring. But the wire holds them securely, so that if something should bump into them, they won't topple over.

Fasten the candles with a few drops of melted candle wax. Cover wire with sprigs of evergreen or strands of princess pine.

For the center, choose the largest apple you can find, scoop out the stem, and wedge a tall candle in the hole by using sprigs of evergreen.

You can achieve a color scheme to suit your holiday décor by the kind of apples you choose—red or yellow, or even green; by the kind of evergreens you use; and by the color of the candles you select. Use red apples with red or white (or both) candles and very green evergreens such as cryptomeria, white pine, balsam; use yellow apples and yellow or white candles with yellowish-green foliage; green apples and blue candles with bluish-green evergreens.

If there is a fire flickering in your fireplace, toss in a few scraps of apple peel and some twigs of evergreen—they will give a lovely aroma!

 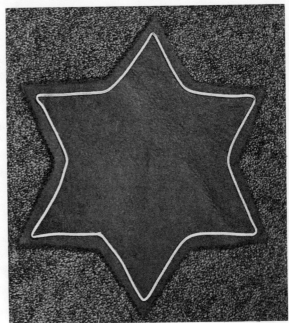

FELT STAR-SHAPED CENTERPIECE

Your coffee table takes on a festive air with a Christmas-star centerpiece made of felt. And your hot coffeepot can sit right on it. Here are three to choose from. The one on the coffee table is green, the one with a Christmas star in each point is white, and the one edged with a single band of gold braid is red.

Start with a Square

For the green mat I used a piece of felt 18 inches square. From a piece of newspaper (also 18 inches square) I cut a pattern for a six-pointed star. (See Chapter VI for directions for making a six-pointed star.) With pinking scissors I cut the star out of the green felt.

Glue gold braid around the star about ½ inch in from the edge. Use Pritt Glue Stick or one of the other stick glues. Decorate the corners of the star with clusters of sequins. A touch of glue will fasten them to the felt.

For the white felt centerpiece, start with a 14-inch square. Cut in the shape of a six-pointed star, glue gold braid around it, and decorate the corners with Christmas stars made of gold braid, tacked on with glue.

The Christmas star has four pieces—the longest (in the middle) is 3 inches long; the two shorter ones are 2½ inches long; and the crosspiece is 1 inch long.

The red centerpiece is 12 inches across and is made in the same fashion, trimmed with one band of gold braid.

Once you have your pattern cut, the mats are quickly made. If you like to use your dining table with place mats instead of a tablecloth, make a star-shaped felt place mat for each member of the family, and use them for Christmas breakfast or midnight supper on Christmas Eve.

☆

CHAPTER V

CANDLELIGHT

This is the time for reverence and reverie—when all the candles are lighted and the soft glow and flickering flame cast their magic spell. This is the time for peaceful thoughts and quiet conversations, a time for contemplation and contentment at the end of a bustling day.

The magic spell of candlelight is more than just myth. It softens tongues and tempers and reduces the decibels. It casts shadows and creates colors that were not there before. As the candles are lighted we pause to reflect on the fascination of the flickering flame, and before we know it we're caught in the magic mood.

Here are some suggestions for candleholders to add to your collection. Most of them can be stored away and brought out year after year.

CHRISTMAS-TREE SCONCE

The Christmas-tree sconce for the wall over the sofa, or beside a tip-top table in a hall, or over the party buffet table is made of aluminum. When the candle is lighted the aluminum gives a soft glow like pewter.

This sconce is 7 inches high, with a 2-inch shelf to hold the candle. Cut a newspaper pattern first, following the diagram given. Trace around your pattern with a pencil on a sheet of aluminum. Cut with regular household scissors and smooth the edges with sandpaper or an emery board.

Bend up the shelf of the sconce, as indicated on the diagram by the dotted line. Polish the sconce with extra-fine steel wool—very gently. This will give it the soft look of pewter.

For the candleholder, cut a piece of aluminum as shown in the sketch. Bend up the four side pieces, as indicated by the dotted lines, leaving about a square inch in the center for the candle to sit on. Attach the candleholder to the center of the shelf with Le Page's liquid solder. Let it dry overnight before you try to put a candle in it, and the bond will hold.

With a nail, make a small hole at the top of the sconce and hang it on the wall. Or attach the sconce to the wall with a Scotch Brand Mounting Square. These hold so well that one would be sufficient for the sconce. Be sure to follow directions on the package. Trim with sprigs of long-needled pine, juni-

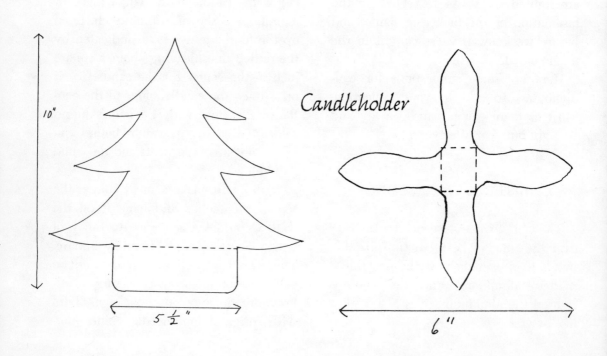

Candleholder

10"

5 ½ "

6 "

per, yew, or whatever you have in your garden, light your candle—and let it cast its spell!

FLEUR-DE-LIS SCONCE

The fleur-de-lis sconce is made in the same fashion as the Christmas-tree sconce. This one is 7½ inches high, with a shelf 2½ inches wide.

Using the sketch as a guide, cut a pattern of newspaper, trace it on the aluminum sheet with a pencil, and cut with scissors. Smooth the rough edges, bend up the shelf, and attach a candle-holder made like the one for the Christmas-tree sconce. (See sketch.)

Store your sconces away for the next Christmas season. They will soon become a tradition in your holiday décor.

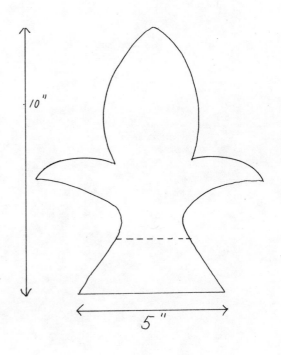

TRIPTYCH SCONCE

The triptych sconce can stand on a table or a desk, or it can hang on a wall to send its triple glow into the room. It is made of aluminum just as the tree and fleur-de-lis sconces are made.

Cut a pattern of newspaper, using the sketches as a guide, and proceed as with the others. Bend along all dotted lines of the sconce as indicated, and stand it up. Polish gently with fine steel wool.

For the shelf, a separate piece of aluminum is attached, to make a smooth surface for the candleholders. Cut the shelf according to the dimensions given (draw the shelf with pencil and ruler on the aluminum first), and attach to the sconce with liquid solder, which comes ready to spread, like glue.

The candleholders for this sconce are square, as shown in the diagram. Cut according to dimensions given. (Again, draw on aluminum with pencil and ruler first.) Bend along the five dotted lines to form a candleholder like the one shown in the sketch.

Secure the candleholders on the shelf, using liquid solder, and center each one so that each panel of the triptych will have a candle in front of it.

Trim with evergreens, and light it for Christmas Eve and every eve till Twelfth-night. Use 5- or 6-inch candles.

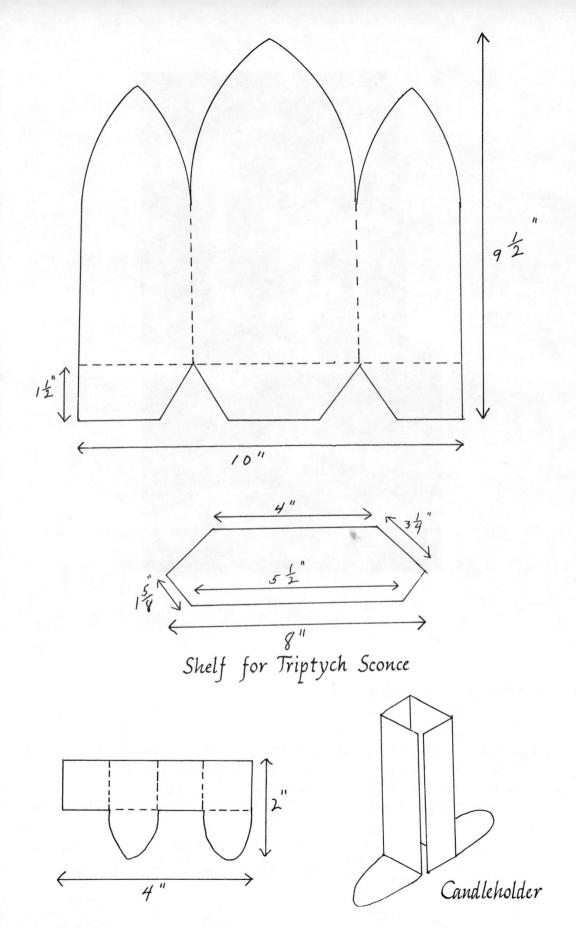

$9\frac{1}{2}$"

$1\frac{1}{2}$"

10"

4"

$3\frac{1}{4}$"

$5\frac{1}{2}$"

$1\frac{5}{8}$"

8"

Shelf for Triptych Sconce

2"

4"

Candleholder

WINEGLASSES AND CANDLES

Many of us collect tiny creatures and figures on our travels, and often these treasures enhance the Christmas scene. If they are too tiny for the Christmas village—or if you are not planning a village—put them under glass. Turn a wineglass over them, or a liqueur glass or a goblet, depending on the size of the figurine. Fasten a candle to the glass with wax or floral clay, and trim with evergreen. A grouping of such glasses, all with treasures underneath and candles on top, can be an effective centerpiece for the dining table or decoration for the mantel. Mix up the sizes so that the candles are not all the same height.

CANDLES AND GOBLETS

Goblets become candleholders when they are turned upside down. Stand them in a row on a wide window sill. Let them light the living room, lined up along the mantel. March them down the middle of the *smörgåsbord* table. They are bright and effective and very quick and easy to arrange.

Inside each goblet, place a large Christmas ball, each one a different color. Secure 10-inch red candles to the bottoms of the goblets (which are now the tops) with candle wax or floral clay. If you use clay, hide it with sprigs of evergreen. If you use candle wax, decorate or not as you wish—the wax matches the candle and does not show.

LUCIA, THE QUEEN OF LIGHT

Lucia Dagen, or Lucia's Day, is celebrated in Scandinavia on the thirteenth of December to welcome in the Christmas season—the season of light.

Lucia (pronounced Loo-see'-a) is the Queen of Light. She dresses in a long white robe and wears a crown of lighted candles on her head, as she walks from room to room at dawn, carrying a tray of coffee and rolls to all the members of the family.

Traditionally, Lucia's crown contained real candles, but today the candles are electrified—like little flashlights.

In many of the offices in Scandinavia today the custom is followed. Sometime during the day, on the thirteenth of December, Lucia comes with lighted crown and a tray of rolls and coffee.

Here we have a 12-inch doll to celebrate Lucia Dagen. Her robe is made of white silk, and her crown holds seven 3½-inch candles. It is made on an embroidery hoop 4 inches in diameter—which just fits her head. The candles, evenly spaced, are attached with masking tape. Princess pine is wound around the hoop and held in place with very fine wire.

We rarely light her candles—unless we are watching carefully—but she stands in the hall to greet our guests as a symbol of the season of light.

LUCIA CROWN

The old-fashioned Lucia crown is easier to use as a centerpiece than as a headpiece! This one came from Stockholm. The large department store in the center of Stockholm, Nordiske Kompaniet, sells these all year round. So if your travels take you to Sweden in mid-summer, you can get Lucia's crown.

The crown holds seven 5½-inch candles (the usual number) in little holders attached to an inch-wide metal band. Decorated with evergreens, it goes well on a large coffee table or as a dining-table centerpiece with a small bouquet inside the ring.

It also fits well on the head, cushioned with a white lace handkerchief. The metal band is made so that it is adjustable to fit all head sizes. But unless you have your own personal fire brigade in attendance, you'll be wiser not to light the crown!

CHRISTMAS CHANDELIER

The Christmas chandelier—a traditional design in traditional colors.

Attach three 5-inch candles, equally spaced, to the outside of an 8-inch embroidery hoop, using masking tape to secure them. Tie three narrow (¼-inch) red satin ribbons to the hoop at the points where the candles are attached—ribbons about 15 inches long. Tie the ends together in a tight knot, making sure the chandelier is level. This is the hardest part of the whole job!

Princess pine is wound around the hoop and fastened with very fine wire that comes on a spool. This pine is on the conservation list in many states, but if you pick it on private property or just ahead of the bulldozer, you will be doing the pine no harm. Mine was gathered on a woodsy hillside at the home of friends in Connecticut.

Hang the chandelier from the ceiling or on a wall bracket above a buffet. For instructions on how to make the wall bracket, see the chapter on mobiles.

Light your candles *only* if your pine is very fresh and green or if it has been sprayed with a fire-deterrent spray, and *only* if you keep an eye on them. The pine burns easily when it is dry.

ANGEL RING WITH CANDLES

The combination of copper and gold gives an illusion of antiquity. Add to this the glow of candlelight and you have a luster of a very special kind.

These angels are made of copper; the ring is covered with gold braid. Each angel holds a 3½-inch white candle.

First, tie three pieces of gold braid, each about 15 inches long, to a 6-inch wooden embroidery hoop, spacing the cords evenly around the hoop. Secure with Sobo glue, and tie the ends in a firm knot. Make sure the ring hangs level.

Next, wind gold braid around the hoop, fastening it with glue as you go

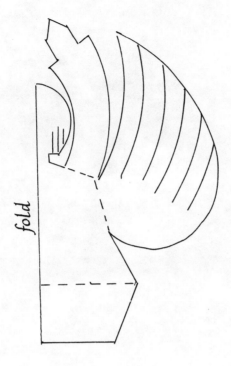

fold

along. Take a bit of care each time you come to one of the cords that have already been tied to the hoop, smoothing the braid carefully over the knots.

Next, from a sheet of 36-gauge copper, cut out three angels, making a pattern from the one given here. (Do not fold the copper, only the pattern.) The copper cuts very easily, even with manicure scissors.

Cut along all lines on wings and head. With the points of embroidery scissors or with very small pointed pliers, roll up the strips on each side of the head to form curls.

Bend up candle shelf and bend wings

back, as indicated by dotted lines on the pattern. For candleholders, cut strips of copper ½ inch wide and 1½ inches long. Roll around the candle to get the proper size, and fasten to the center of candle shelf with liquid solder.

After the solder has thoroughly dried, fasten the angels to the hoop, one between each golden cord, with Sobo glue. For extra security, run a single strand of gold cord around the hoop, letting it go between the body of the angel and the candleholder. Fasten it with glue.

Place candles in the candleholders, fold arms down around candles—and your angel ring is complete.

ANGEL
HOLDING TWO CANDLES

This angel can be made of either copper or aluminum. The copper is easier to cut, but on the other hand, the aluminum is sturdier and much less likely to be dented. Once having fashioned an aluminum angel, you'll have her for many a year.

The color, of course, will be quite different, depending on whether you choose copper or aluminum—one has a luster and the other a silvery gleam.

Use the pattern given here, and trace around it on the metal with a pencil. If you use aluminum, cut with house-hold scissors. And remember that rough or jagged edges can be smoothed out with sandpaper. If you use copper, cut with embroidery scissors.

Cut all lines on wings and head. Roll curls forward and down toward the face. Carefully turn the disks that hold the candles so they are horizontal. Bend arms and wings as indicated by dotted lines on the pattern and bend the skirt to form a cone.

Cut strips of metal, ¾ inch by ½ inch, and curl them around the candle to get the proper size. Attach them to the disks with liquid solder.

The candles will burn for only twenty minutes, but they are easily replaced.

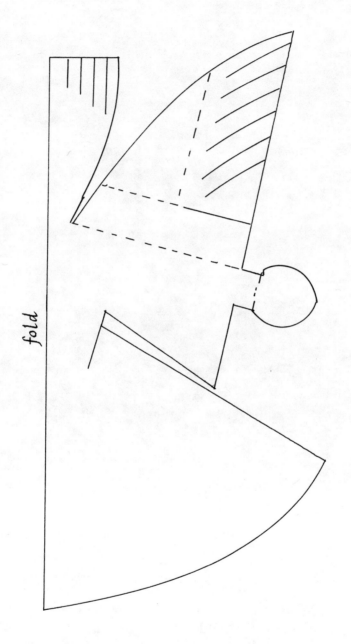

ANGEL
HOLDING A SINGLE CANDLE

This angel, too, can be made of copper or of aluminum. Cut according to the pattern given and cut all lines on wings and head. Bend along dotted lines. Roll the curls forward and down toward the face. Fasten a circle of metal between the hands to hold the candle. I use a 3½-inch candle for this one.

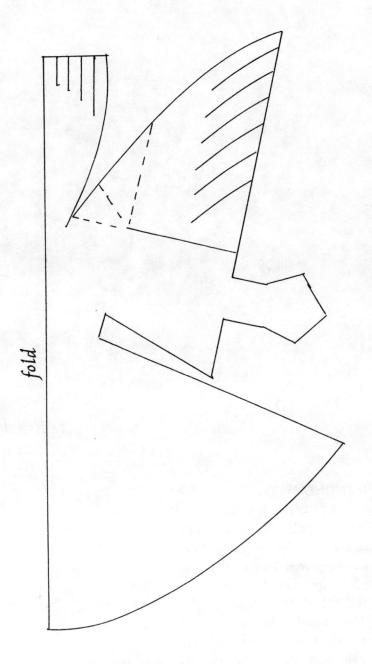

fold

Candleholder

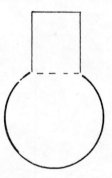

COPPER ANGEL WITH CANDLE

This circular angel, cut out of copper, carries a candle on her skirt. Follow the pattern given. You will notice that the wings are slotted so that one fits into the other, thus holding the angel together. Feather her wings and roll up her curls. Cut out the disk that holds the candle, following the pattern given. Bend it up along dotted line and fasten it to the skirt at the shaded area in the sketch. Use liquid solder. Cut a

½-inch strip large enough to go around the base of a 3½-inch candle and secure it to the disk. Bend arms down around the candle.

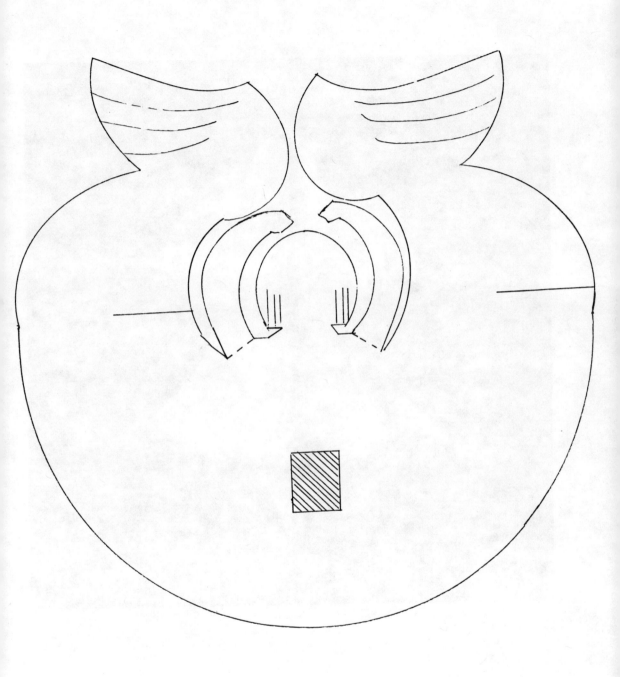

☆

CHAPTER VI

DECORATIONS THAT HANG

P aper and foil are the most popular
materials for making decorations
that hang. All the shades and hues of
the rainbow are available in these materials—and color is half the fun of making decorations. Make the same decoration in, say, red and blue, and then
make it in yellow and green, and the
one will appear to be quite different
from the other.

Circles and squares, stars and strips—
all the geometric shapes are used. And
they should be cut as accurately as possible to give the decoration a proper
finish, a perfect balance, and a pleas-
ing proportion.

To cut a circle use a compass to draw
a pattern—if you have a compass. If you
do not have a compass, tie a string to
the point of a pencil and use as you
would a compass. Hold the string with
one finger at the center point and draw
your circle just as you would with a
compass.

Simpler than that is to find a saucer,
a bowl, or a cup of about the size you
want, and trace around it. You can also
cut a circle from a square by folding the
square in half and then in half again,
and then making a curved cut from
one corner to the corner opposite it,

eliminating the point that has no folded
edges. Fold as shown in the sketch and
cut along the broken line.

The easiest way to cut a star shape
is to follow a pattern. But sometimes
the pattern you have will not give you
a star of the size you want; in that case
you must make a pattern for your star.

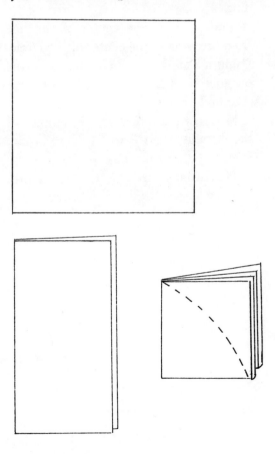

79

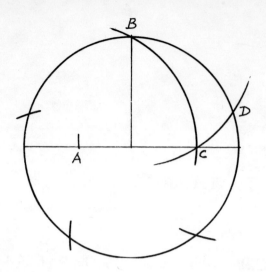

To draw a five-pointed star, follow the diagram given here. You will need a compass.

First, make the circle and draw in the diameter and the perpendicular radius.

Find point *A*, the center of the line from the edge to the center of the circle. Using a radius on your compass of the distance from *A* to *B*, swing an arc from *A* to find point *C*.

Next, using a radius on the compass of the distance from *B* to *C*, swing an arc from *B* to find point *D*.

The distance from *B* to *D* is a fifth of the circle—use this measurement to find the five equally distant points around the circle.

Draw lines between the points, and you'll have your star.

A six-pointed star is simpler to make. Cut a circle of paper. Fold it in half and then fold in thirds, and then fold in half again. Cut along dotted line as shown in the diagram. Open it up and you have a six-pointed star.

Many of the decorations that follow can be folded up and packed away for the next season.

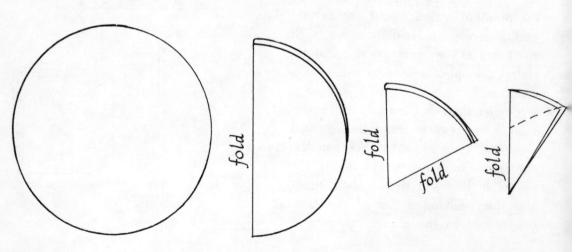

PUFF BALL

Puff balls in white or in vibrant colors will trim your tree with distinction.

Start with a Circle

Cut twelve 3-inch circles of the paper and color of your choice. (You can use tissue paper, gold wrapping paper, shelf paper, or plain white bond, and use twice as many circles if you choose tissue paper.)

Without making any crease except just at the point, fold each circle in half and then in half again. The whole secret of making the puff ball is to make segments without creases.

Using strong thread—preferably nylon—sew through the corner of each segment, as shown in the diagram. Secure the knot by sewing twice through the first segment. If you are making your puff ball of tissue paper, sew through a tiny circle of cardboard before stringing

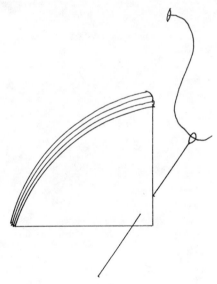

the segments on the thread, and then finish with another tiny piece. Otherwise, the thread may tear the delicate paper.

Pull thread up tight to form a ball. Fasten securely by sewing once more through the last segment, and suspend the ball by the same thread.

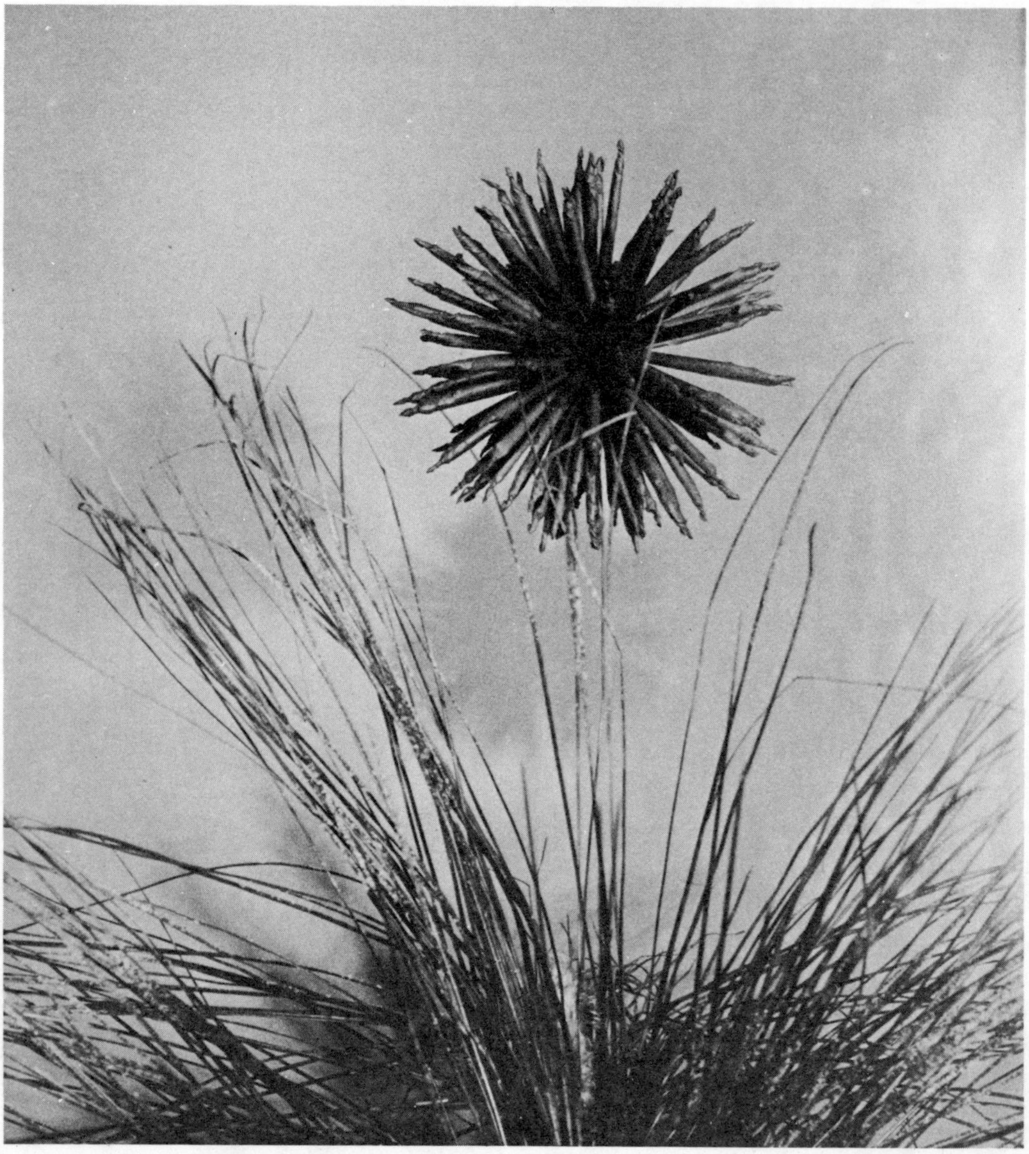

SWEDISH TISSUE-PAPER BALL

The Swedish tissue-paper ball is effective on a Christmas tree, or suspended in a doorway, where it will twirl with the air currents.

Start with a Circle

Cut twenty-five circles (cut several at a time) about 5 inches in diameter. Divide each circle into six equal parts (fold in half and then into thirds, and make strong creases), and cut to within an inch of the center. (See next page.)

Roll each segment from one side to the other over a ⅜-inch dowel or a slim pencil. (Sometimes I use a nut pick!) Twist the tip, and slip out the dowel. It is simple to do, but time-consuming, as you can see, and it does require a bit of patience.

Each circle will give you six spikes, and no glue is necessary. When the segments of all twenty-five circles are rolled up, sew through the center of each circle, starting and ending with a tiny circle of cardboard so as not to tear the fragile tissue paper. Pull thread up tight to form a round ball, and fasten thread. Suspend by the same thread.

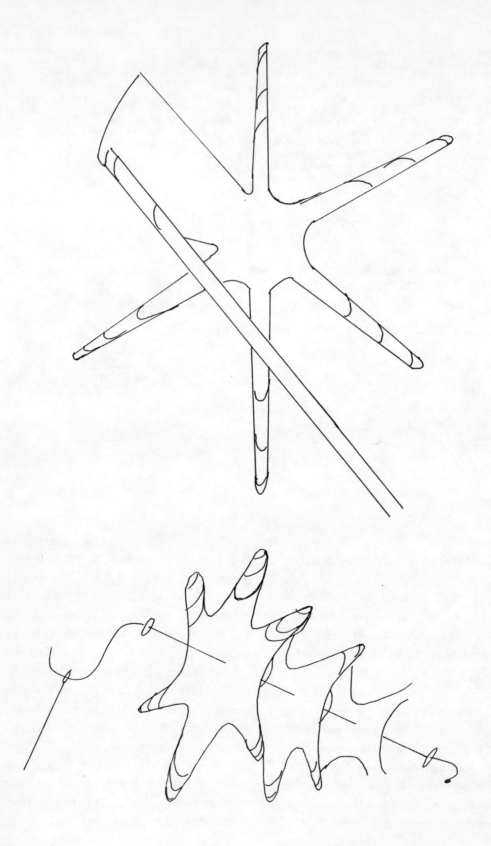

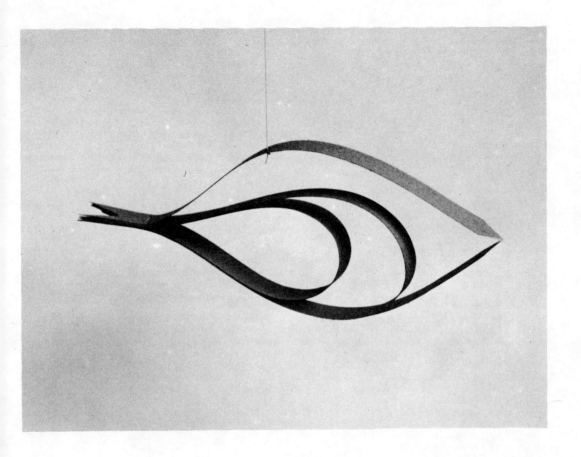

FISH

Paper of some rigidity, such as construction paper, works very well for the fish. I usually make mine in two colors.

Start with a Strip

The fish takes three strips, each ¾ inch wide: one 17 inches long, one 14 inches long, and one 11 inches long. This will give you a fish 8 inches long.

Fold the longest strip in half and crease the fold. Bend the other two strips in half but do not crease, thus forming loops. Place the shortest strip—looped—inside the next—also looped. Place the longest strip on the outside. Make sure all the ends are evenly matched (all six of them) and staple them together about 1½ inches from the end. Notch the tail (the stapled end) and make a point for the nose, without cutting off so much that the fish will be cut in two.

Suspend by a thread, experimenting to find out just where the thread should be so that your fish will be properly balanced. The fish should swim horizontally, and since the tail is heavier than the nose, the thread should be slightly off-center, toward the tail.

Make a mobile of three, five, or seven fish, using fish that are about half as large, but made in the same proportion. For instructions, see the chapter on mobiles.

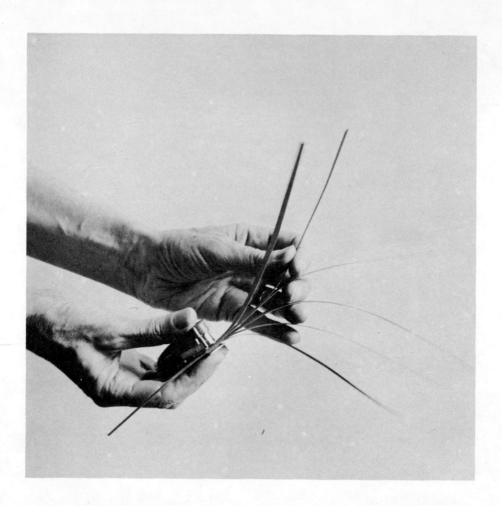

HEART TWIRLER

Red is the obvious color for the heart, but it is effective in other colors too. Use construction paper or metallic foil.

Start with a Strip

First, cut seven strips, each about ½ inch wide, in these lengths: two strips 9 inches; two 7½ inches; two 6 inches; and one (for the center) 4 inches. This gives you three pairs and a single one for the stem.

Second, arrange the strips for sta-

pling: Hold the 4-inch strip (which goes down through the center of the heart) downward. All the others are held upward and are graduated on either side of the center strip—the longest ones are placed on either side of the center strip, then the next size, and finally the 6-inch size on the outside. Staple through all seven strips, as shown in the photograph.

Third, pull all the strips down, three on each side of the center stem, making sure the ends are all even with the bottom of the center strip. Staple securely. Suspend by a thread.

[14] The little church nestles into the hillside surrounded by *tomtes* and an angel and several table-size trees. For instructions, see Chapter II.

[15] The village church is made in two sections, for easy storing. Patterns and instructions for making the church are given in Chapter II.

[16] Christmas *tomtes* (sprites) admire the little glitter tree. They are made of paper cones. For details and instructions, see Chapter II.

[17] The Wise Men arrive at the village barn. Instructions for making these figures and the barn with its silo are given in Chapter II.

[18] The Christmas cross from Sweden, hand-carved from a single piece of wood, stands beside a group of four gold-foil angels. For instructions, see Chapter VII.

[19] Tree of Christmas balls makes the buffet centerpiece or trims the hallway table. It is made on a knitting needle. For instructions, see Chapter IV.

[20] Three small golden angels are grouped on a hall table with a tiny tree. See Chapter VII.

[21] The harlequin angel accents the greenery along a balcony railing. Details are given in Chapter VII. Instructions for making the little white mouse are given in Chapter II.

[23] A centerpiece of apples, big and small, holds nine candles and is decorated with sprigs of evergreen. For instructions, see Chapter IV.

[22] The Wise Men are greeted by the donkey and *tomtes,* as they march along the ledge of a stairway. See Chapter II.

[24] Place cards that stand upright, made from Christmas-card cutouts, dress up the party table. For instructions, see Chapter IX.

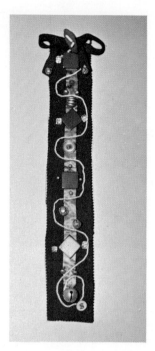

[25] A treasure *klockasträng* for the door is made of trinkets and treasures, bells and gold braid. For details, see Chapter III.

[26] A crèche for the mantel, or under the Christmas tree, has figures of Christmas-card cutouts. Instructions are given in Chapter IX.

[27] An asymmetrical treasure box trimmed with lace holds many small souvenirs from Europe. The details are given in Chapter VII.

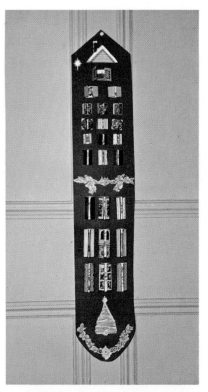

[28] An Advent calendar in the form of a *klockasträng* is made with last year's Christmas cards. For details, see Chapter IX.

[29] A ring of copper angels holding candles is suspended over the copper coffeepot. See Chapter V for instructions.

[30] Orange-juice cans, painted gold and tied with red bows and evergreen boughs, give glamour to the kitchen door. Details are given in Chapter III.

[31] Strips of felt cut with pinking scissors and trimmed with sleigh bells and gold cowbell make an old-fashioned *klockasträng*. See Chapter III.

[32] A medieval screen, in the form of a triptych, combines reproductions of famous paintings with plain gold paper and gold cord. For details, see Chapter IX.

[34] The frosty look of the snowball tree makes a wintry scene for a hallway table. For complete details, see Chapter IV.

[33] Holly rings, tied with red velvet, make a traditional decoration for a hallway or stairwell. See Chapter III.

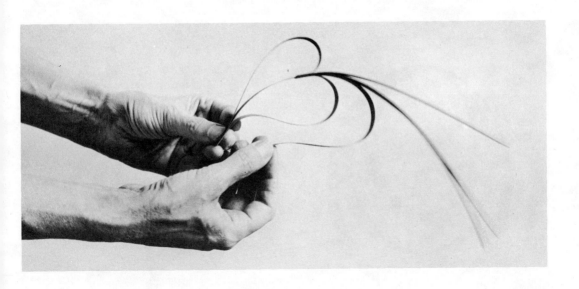

SINGLE TWIRLER

I used two colors for my single twirler —Chinese red and moss green. But you can make it all of a shade, gold and silver, green and blue, or choose a different color for each strip. Some rigidity is needed to make the strips bow properly. Use metallic foil, colored construction paper, or Bristol board.

THE THREE RINGS

Loops within loops, and each in a different color, can be suspended in a doorway or on a Christmas tree. Metallic foil or construction paper is good for this one.

Start with a Strip

Cut three strips ¾ inch wide, each one in a different color, in these lengths: 18 inches, 15 inches, and 12 inches.

With the shortest strip on top, then the next, and finally the longest, match all the ends, lap them over about ½ inch, staple them together. Suspend by a black thread.

Start with a Strip

All seven strips are the same width: ¾ inch. The center one measures 5½ inches long, the next two (one on each side of the center one) are 6 inches long, and the outside strips are 7 inches long.

Match ends, top and bottom, staple them together, and suspend by a thread.

DOUBLE TWIRLER

Double twirlers are excellent breeze-catchers. I used blue, red and yellow for mine, which gives the decoration a sort of country-cousin look. It's reminiscent of the designs one finds on furniture in the Pennsylvania Dutch countryside and in the mountains of Norway.

Start with a Strip

The center strip is 8½ inches long.

The next two are 10 inches long; the next two are 11½ inches long; and the outside strips are 13 inches long. All are ¾ inch wide.

Make sure the two matching strips (the two outer ones, the next two, etc.) are exactly the same length, so the twirl will not be lopsided.

Staple ends together, top and bottom, making sure they all meet exactly.

Then staple all strips together just below the mid-point of the center stem, making the double bow. Suspend by a thread.

SEGMENTED CHRISTMAS BALL

Red or green construction paper, gold or silver metallic foil are ideal for the segmented Christmas ball.

Start with a Circle

Out of the paper of your choice cut nine circles 4 inches in diameter. Fold each circle in half and crease them through the center. Open them up, stack them together, and on the crease staple them together at top, at bottom, and in the middle.

Alternating top and bottom, fasten together with a small dab of glue the outer edges of the segments about a third of the way down (and up). Run a thread through the center top of all nine circles —and hang it up.

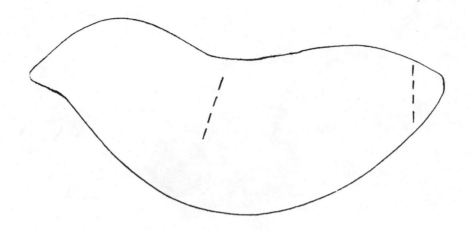

SWEDISH CHRISTMAS BIRD

The Swedish Christmas bird is traditionally suspended over the Christmas dinner table, bringing good luck to the household.

Follow the pattern given here. It was sent to me from Sweden many years ago. The body of the bird is made of Bristol board or cardboard. The wings and tail are tissue paper. Cut two strips, each 5 inches wide and 9 inches long. Fold and snip the strips exactly as with the snowflake that is in this chapter.

Make two slits in the body, as indicated by the broken lines in the pattern. With manicure scissors (or embroidery scissors), widen each slit to about 1/16 inch so that the wings and tail can be slipped through.

Secure both sides of the wings and tail to the body with small pieces of cellophane tape. Spread out the wings. Fasten the center of the tail together with cellophane tape so that it forms a

semicircle. Suspend the bird by a thread run through the body at a point off-center toward the back, making sure the bird is properly balanced. You may have to experiment to find the balance point.

The birds are made in all colors and in white.

PAPER ANGEL

An angel of paper to hang in a doorway—simple to make. She really floats, whether she is made of gold foil or colored construction paper.

Cut one body and two wings, using the patterns given here. Choose one color for the angel body and another for the wings. My angel is blue and she has chartreuse wings.

Staple or glue wings to body, with the points of the wings facing toward the head and one wing slightly forward of the other. Bend wings out from the body a little so that the angel becomes three-dimensional. Run a thread through the body—experimenting until you find the right spot so she will balance—and hang her up. If you want to keep her for another year, fold the wings together and place her in the bottom of the Christmas box.

Three angels, each of a different color or all of gold or silver, can be attached to wires to make a mobile. (For instructions, see the chapter on mobiles.)

TRADITIONAL BIRD

One of the nicest symbols of the Christmas season is the bird—a reminder of the new year to come. Here's a simple one to make.

Cut out one body and two wings, using the pattern given here. Make your bird of construction paper or metallic foil, with the body of one color and the wings of another. Staple the wings to the body (or use glue) and bend wings slightly away from the body. Suspend by a thread run through the body. Make sure your bird will balance—if the thread is too far back, his head will drop!

Three, five, or seven birds can be used for a mobile. For instructions, see the chapter on mobiles.

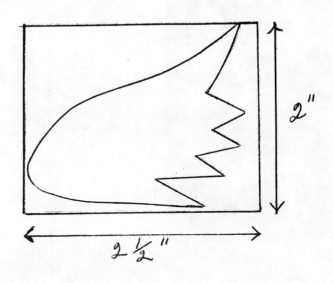

2"

2 ½"

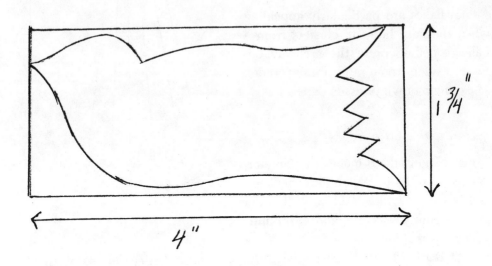

1 ¾"

4"

SNOWFLAKE

Snowflakes are particularly appealing when they are hung in clusters from a hallway ceiling or in the archway between living room and dining room. Make them of white tissue paper.

Start with a Strip

For a snowflake 6 inches in diameter, cut a strip of tissue paper 18 inches long and 6 inches wide. Fold in half, then in half again, and again, and so on until your strip is folded up to a width of ½ inch. Crease the folds carefully, open up the strip, and then, using the creases as a guide, refold in accordion pleats.

When the strip is again folded up to a width of ½ inch, staple in the middle, across the width. (See sketch.) Snip out tiny triangular pieces on each side of the folded strip, as shown in the dia-

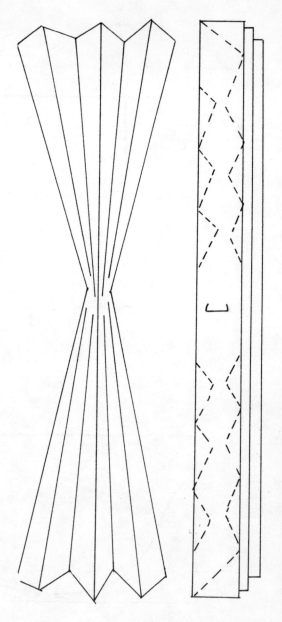

gram, and cut points on the ends. Each snowflake you make should be snipped a little differently, because, as you know, snowflakes are never alike.

Open up to form a circle and fasten the sides together with cellophane tape. Suspend by a thread slipped through one of the triangular cutouts.

SEGMENTED PAPER BELL

Many kinds of paper and foil are good to use for the paper bell. Plain white bond is especially effective.

Start with a Rectangle

Out of fifteen rectangles 4½ inches by 5 inches, cut fifteen bells, following the pattern given. Fold each bell in half and make a strong crease. Flatten out the bells, stack them up, and staple three times along the crease, at top, at bottom, and in the middle. Gently fold each segment away from the next until the bell is completely opened up. Run a thread through the top of the bell, and hang it up.

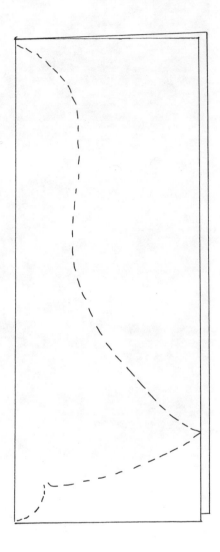

SIX-POINTED PAPER STAR

First cut a pattern for a six-pointed star, following directions given at the beginning of this chapter.

Start with a Square

Out of fifteen squares, cut fifteen stars, and make your decoration just as the bell is made.

You can go right on, making all kinds of shapes in this fashion—a five-pointed star, a heart, a snowball. Make up your own patterns or follow some of those given here. Be sure your design is symmetrical so it will hang properly, and fill your tree with paper balls, all of a color or all colors of the rainbow. I like to make them of plain white bond paper (regular typing paper). They look crisp and snowy.

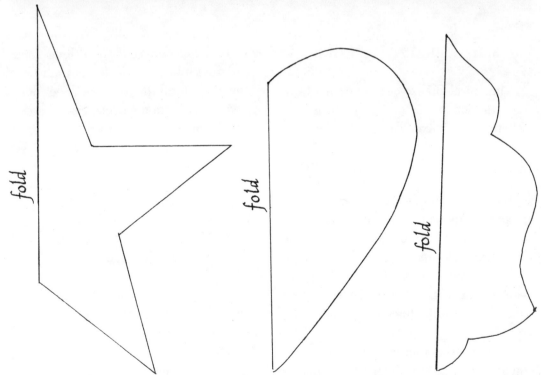

SPIRAL BREEZE-CATCHER

The spiral breeze-catcher is made of construction paper or Bristol board, in whatever color you like.

Start with a Circle

Using a compass, draw a circle 6 inches in diameter. Within this circle, draw circles ½ inch apart, until you have six circles in all, as in the diagram. With a pencil and ruler, very lightly divide in quarters, as shown. These quarter lines will be guidelines in sketching the spirals.

Each of the four spirals starts at a quarter mark. Sketch carefully before you start to cut. Your spiral lines should progress inward ½ inch per quarter, all the way into the center. (See dotted lines in diagram.) You can erase on both construction paper and Bristol board, so if your curves do not suit you, try again!

Cut around outside circle. Then cut along dotted lines, using manicure scissors, until you have four separate spirals. Suspend a paper ball (see Chapter VI for instructions on how to make it) or a small Christmas ball in the center, and hang the breeze-catcher by a thread. Place it where there are air currents and it will spin slowly and constantly, and you'll find it's an eye-catcher as well as a breeze-catcher!

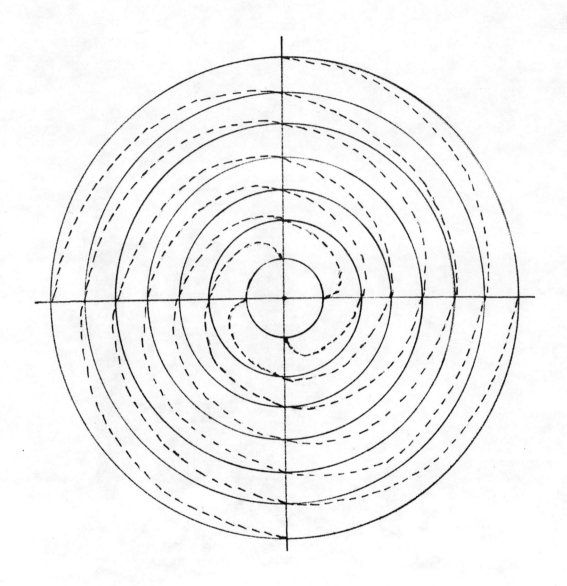

CHAPTER VII

SPECIAL FEATURES

Included in this section are decorations that can dominate the décor, the features that might become highlights of your Christmas trimmings.

Sometimes one feature is all we want, and if we find just the right wreath for the window, or exactly the star for the stairway, our trimmings are complete. Here are a few suggestions.

A CHRISTMAS CRÈCHE
FROM THE WORLD OF THE EAST

From the eastern parts of Europe comes the design for this Christmas crèche. It imitates the towers and turrets of a fairyland castle and the colorful spires of cathedrals to be found only in the Old World.

The crèche is made mostly of recycled materials: seven tin cans, cardboard, a plastic egg (the kind that contains hosiery), colored construction paper, gold paint, and fast-drying enamel.

Start with two 12-ounce cans, the kind that soup comes in. These are the largest (4½ inches tall, 2½ inches across) and stand at the bottom of the crèche. Paint these two cans red, using fast-drying enamel. Decorate one side of each with colorful cutouts, either from last year's Christmas cards or cut from colored construction paper. Attach with white glue.

Next, place the two decorated cans 4 inches apart on your work table (don't put them on the base of the crèche until the last thing), and across the tops of the cans glue a platform of heavy cardboard (I used corrugated cardboard) 10½ inches long and 3½ inches wide. Paint the platform with red enamel and trim the edges with red bias tape, glued in place with white glue. With a fine brush, decorate the tape with a zigzag line of gold paint.

Next comes the second tier of cans. These are small vegetable cans—8½ ounces—3 inches tall, 2½ inches across. Paint these gold and decorate the front of each with colorful cutouts. Then glue these two cans to the long platform just over the two cans below.

On each of these 8½-ounce cans, glue a platform of cardboard 3½ inches square. Paint with red and trim the edges with red bias tape. Paint a zigzag gold line on the tapes.

In the center of the crèche is a typical "onion-top" tower so familiar to Eastern architecture. To make this tower, start with a 3½-ounce tuna-fish

can. Paint it gold and decorate it with a round medallion, perhaps one that you might find on your old Christmas cards.

Next, make a cone of red construction paper, using two-thirds of a circle 6 inches in diameter. Cut off the *bottom* 1¼ inches of the cone, trim it with gold zigzag lines, and glue it to the top of the tuna-fish can. The cone has an open top into which the egg will fit.

Paint the plastic egg with red enamel, paint zigzag gold lines around the middle of it, and then glue it into the open-topped cone.

Make another red-construction-paper cone to put on top of the egg. This one

is made with a quarter of a circle 8 inches in diameter, to give you a tall, narrow cone. Glue it to the top of the egg, and again paint gold zigzag lines, this time around the bottom of the cone.

The two top cans are frozen-orange-juice cans, each 4 inches tall and 2 inches across. Paint these gold, decorate with cutouts, and glue to the centers of the two square cardboard platforms. Their towers are made of colored construction paper, actually one cone inside another. (I used pastel colors for mine.)

First, make two wide cones, using two-thirds of a circle 6 inches in diameter. Cut off the *top* 1¼ inches of the cone, and glue this to the top of the can.

Then make two more cones, using a quarter of a circle 8 inches in diameter, and glue these narrow cones on top of the wide, short ones. Decorate these towers with gold paint, using a fine brush.

Snip off about ¼ inch of the point of these two top cones, and glue a red sourball—the hard candy that comes in cellophane—to each point to finish off the towers.

For the dark blue background between the bottom two cans, cut a piece of construction paper 9 inches long and 4½ inches wide. Glue this to the backs of the cans. On this background, glue three rings of gold paper for the radiating halo. The rings are 3½, 2½, and 2 inches in diameter, each ring about ¼ inch wide.

When your towers are all fastened together and completed, place the crèche on its base, and secure with Elmer's glue. Do this last, so the base won't be damaged as you work on the towers. Before you glue the towers on, paint the

base—which is a cover of a shoe box— with dark green enamel, and trim it with zigzag gold lines.

Finally, stand a crib with the Christ Child (cut from one of your old Christmas cards) in the crèche. For instructions on how to mount the cutout so it will stand, see Chapter IX.

Stand your crèche on your mantel, or the hall table, or put it in your picture window—and watch the children's eyes light up when they see it! My little friend Jason found mine so enchanting he wanted to take it home with him!

A WREATH
AROUND YOUR WINDOW

Last Christmas instead of putting a wreath in the window, I put the window in a wreath. It turned out to be the hit of our holiday decorations.

I started with eight large branches of

long-needled pine and a spool of 22-gauge wire. First, I placed several layers of newspapers on the kitchen floor, roughly drawing with a soft pencil a circle about 60 inches in diameter—my window is a little less than 60 inches square. The newspaper pattern served only as a guide.

Then, following the natural curve of the branches, I wired them together, hiding the wire in the needles at each turn and making the curve of the branches conform to the penciled circle on the newspapers. I wound the wire continuously, not breaking it once, until the entire wreath was finished.

Wear work gloves if you use long-needled pine, as the branches are covered with pitch.

When the wreath was finished, it was suspended from the ceiling molding by picture hooks and wire.

In each of the sixteen small panes in the window I hung a sprig of evergreen, each a different kind and each tied with red ribbon. And I sprayed the panes with artificial snow to make it a wintry window.

The evergreens I used were juniper, holly, boxwood, balsam, bayberry, mistletoe, cryptomeria, yew, spruce, hemlock, long-needled pine, azalea, rhododendron, mountain laurel, and two kinds of heather.

A red satin bow on the wreath and a Christmas-ball tree on the window sill completed the picture.

LACE-TRIMMED TREASURE BOX

Treasure boxes have become increasingly popular for the display of all kinds of trinkets, trophies, and miniatures, and for the safekeeping of whatever small figurines one collects on one's travels. Some boxes display shells, some minerals and stones, depending on the interests of the collector.

For an easy-to-make treasure box, start with a cardboard box such as a large cereal container. Cut off the front panel, keeping the remainder to make the four sides of the display case, plus its back. If the top has been mutilated in the opening, it can be taped together with masking tape.

To make shelves in the box, cut strips of cardboard as wide as the box is deep and 1 inch longer than the shelf will be. Bend the strip ½ inch at either end, and glue these tabs to the sides of the box so they will secure the shelf in the box.

To make your shelves asymmetrical, build them from the bottom up, each time gluing ½-inch tab to either the side of the box or to the upright strip from which it extends. (See photograph.)

When the form is finished, give the treasure box a coat of fast-drying enamel of whatever color you like, and glue lace to all the edges, using Pritt Glue Stick.

To hang the box on a wall, you can use Scotch Brand Mounting Squares, a new adhesive that sticks very well. It is adhesive on both sides, and four squares will hold a pound of weight. But be careful! This adhesive will take the paint off the wall if you don't follow the directions for its removal.

Your treasure box, if you prefer, can stand on a table—or can be attached to the wall with a conventional hanger.

HEARTS ON THE
BLUEBERRY BRANCH

In Scandinavia the heart is a favorite design at Christmas time. This "tree" is made of a single branch of high-bush blueberry trimmed with 1½-inch red hearts from Sweden, made of very thin wood.

The branch is set in plaster of Paris in a coffee can painted with red enamel and trimmed with gold braid secured with glue.

The hearts can be made of heavy red paper, metallic foil, or balsa wood painted red. And the tree could be used for Christmas or for St. Valentine's Day.

Other branches, of course, can be used, but the blueberry is particularly interesting because of its gnarled and windswept form and its silvery-gray sheen.

THE SNOWMAN

This snowman sits by the fireside and never melts away. He has become a "tradition" with the children in my family, and each year he is refurbished with a fresh layer of snowy cotton.

A ten-pound flour bag is the foundation for the body, a five-pound bag for the head.

Place a ¼-inch dowel 15 inches long in the center of the larger bag and stuff crumpled newspapers around it until the bag is filled. Fill the smaller bag with crumpled newspapers and turn it upside down over the top of the dowel, making sure the bag goes down over the top of the ten-pound bag. Tie string tightly around the two bags where they meet, to make the neck.

Cut off the hook of a wire coat hanger, open up the hanger, and stick it right through bag and newspapers (the larger bag) to form the arms. Turn back wire from each end toward the body, so that the arms are formed of double wire. Tie newspapers (folded) around wire, to give shape to the arms.

Cover the bags and the arms with a thin coating of Sobo glue (a paintbrush dipped in the glue works very well) and put a layer of cotton batting over the entire snowman. A second layer is placed over the first—it will stick without any more glue—and more layers are added until the snowman is built up to the size you want. Mine is 18 inches tall without his hat.

Cut eyes and mouth out of black construction paper and glue in place. Glue on a tiny red Christmas ball for the nose. A wide red satin ribbon makes his scarf.

The snowman's hat is made of black construction paper. Cut an oval shape, roughly 5½ inches by 8 inches, and a strip 6½ inches by 12 inches. Staple the strip (the stovepipe) together and glue it to the oval (the brim). Tie a red metallic-foil bell in one hand. This snowman has a red wooden Swedish bird perched beside his hat.

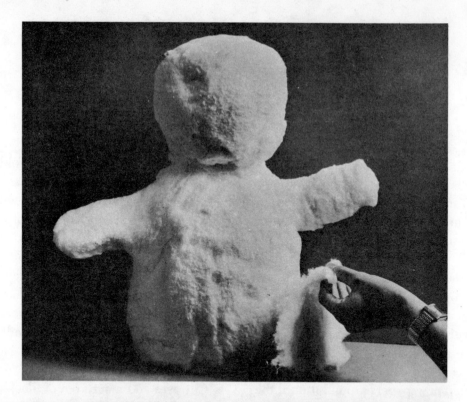

HARLEQUIN ANGEL

An angel without wings is the harlequin angel, and she comes from Scandinavia.

Start with a Circle

Use red construction paper or gold
Christmas wrapping paper. Cut a circle
5 inches in diameter.

Fold the circle in half, and again in
half, and again and again, until the
circle is folded into pie-shaped sections
that measure 1 inch at the outer edge
and taper to a point at the center.

Unfold, and then refold in accordion
pleats, using the first fold marks as a
guide.

Cut a circle 1¾ inches in diameter
of white construction paper (or silver
wrapping paper if you are using gold
wrapping for the body). Through the
center of the white circle and down
through the center of the pleated red
circle, insert the stem of a small silver
Christmas ball—the kind that has a
pipe-cleaner stem.

For the hat, cut a circle of red (or
gold) 3½ inches in diameter. Using
only about a quarter of the circle, form
a cone that will fit the Christmas-ball
head. Staple it together and attach to
the head with a few dabs of glue.

Let the harlequin sit among your
greens, or place her on plate glass to get
the full benefit of her reflected glory.

A CHRISTMAS TREE FOR
THE BIRDS

A sheaf of grain (available in the fall in flower shops that carry dried-plant material) with the largest and fattest kernels to be found, is tied to a pole, trimmed with a large red bow, and placed in the garden. In ancient times it was believed that if your sheaf attracted large numbers of birds at Christmas, your garden would prosper the following season.

Today many city dwellers join in this ancient custom, fastening a sheaf of grain to their balconies, or to the tops of their year-round feeders.

TWELVE-POINTED STAR

The twelve-pointed star is easy to make from gold or silver gift-wrapping paper or from metallic foil of any color. Add it to evergreen branches on your door, use it to accent a stairway festoon, or tie it with ribbons for each side of your mantel and illuminate it with a candle.

Cut two circles, one 6 inches and one 5½ inches in diameter. Divide each circle into six equal parts, as you would a pie, and cut each segment to within an inch of the center of the circle. Cut a ½-inch hole in the center of each circle.

Then form points of each segment by folding back and stapling together (do not crease) the corners of the segment. You will now have two stars, each with six points.

For the center of the star use a colored Christmas ball, or use cranberries as I did. Attach an 8-inch wire (22-gauge) to each of seven cranberries (or to a 1-inch Christmas ball) and twist the wires together. Draw wires through the center hole of the smaller circle and then through the larger circle and through a 1½-inch block of Styrofoam, twisting wire back upon itself to secure. Arrange the points of the star so that they alternate, giving you a twelve-pointed star.

Evergreens may be inserted into the Styrofoam backing block.

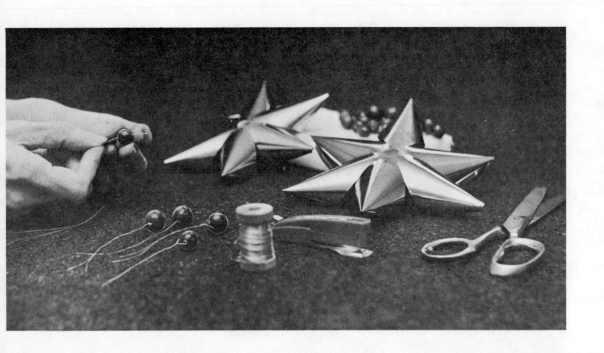

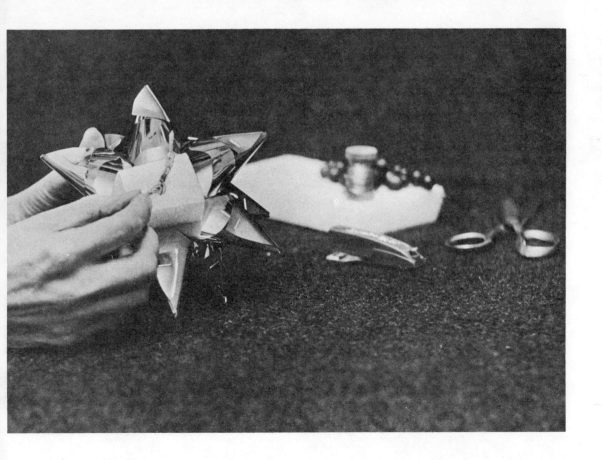

THE CONE ANGEL

Golden angels made of cones can be used in many ways. Here they stand, three together, decorated with cryptomeria.

Start with a Circle

Gold Christmas wrapping paper is good for these. Make the diameter of your circle twice as long as the height you'd like your angel to be. For instance, for an angel 5 inches tall, cut a circle 10 inches in diameter—which is the size of the circle I used for the tallest one shown in the photograph. The medium-sized angel is 3½ inches tall (a 7-inch circle) and the littlest angel is 2¼ inches tall (a 4½-inch circle).

Make a cut from the edge of the circle to the center, overlapping the cut edges to form a cone. Secure with dabs of glue. This way of making a cone (instead of cutting off a third of the circle) gives extra sturdiness to a lightweight paper. It works well with the gold wrapping paper.

Follow the patterns given for the wings. Before you cut, fold the gold paper double, so the wrong sides are on the inside. Cut out the wings and with a toothpick put a few very tiny spots of glue between the two pieces of paper.

Snip off the point of the cone and fasten with glue a silver Christmas ball of about the right size for the head. Attach wings with glue. Make a halo of a piece of gold cord, and glue the halo just above the wings.

If this is the year of the angel, make them of cones—and make them gold!

127

SINGLE ANGEL RING

The angels on the single ring are made of brightly colored foil. Their double wings (see pattern) give them a three-dimensional look. Fold the front wings slightly forward.

Cut the angel bodies according to the pattern given. Cover the halo and feet with a thin coating of Sobo glue and sprinkle with gold or silver glitter. Then glue on the wings—first the smaller ones and then the larger.

Tie three pieces of gold cord, each 15 inches long, to a 6-inch embroidery hoop at evenly spaced intervals, and fasten them in place with glue.

In between the cords, glue the angels to the hoop. Wind princess pine or cryptomeria around the hoop and use very fine wire to hold the pine in place.

Knot the ends of the three pieces of cord together—make sure the angel ring hangs level—and suspend from a wall bracket.

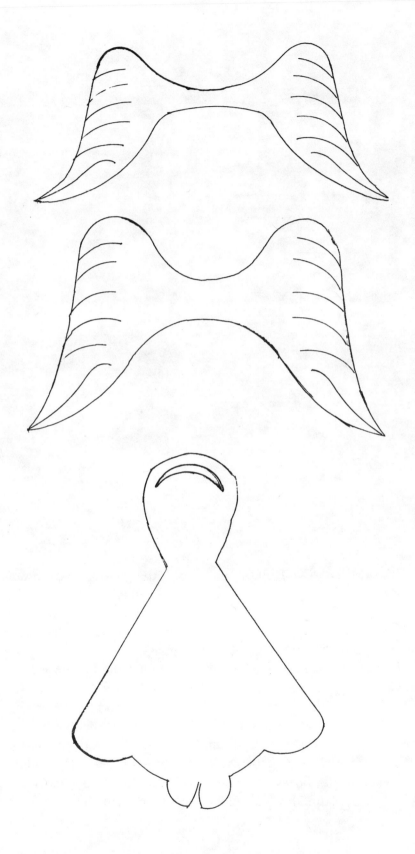

GINGHAM TRINKET BOX

All the compartments in the gingham treasure box are the same size. I used nine individual cereal boxes for mine.

Glue the boxes—with the front panels cut out—onto a piece of cardboard or heavy poster board cut to fit. Then frame the whole with a strip of cardboard as wide as the boxes are deep. Glue white rickrack braid to all edges of the treasure box, using Elmer's or Sobo glue.

Then cover the "frame" with red and white gingham, attaching it with white glue.

Stand the box on a table or fasten it to a wall with Scotch Brand Mounting Squares, and fill the compartments with your finest miniatures.

Use Mounting Squares with care: They will take the paint off the wall when the box is removed unless you follow the directions carefully.

☆

CHAPTER VIII

MOBILES

The changing pattern, the quiet motion, the freely floating forms—these are the qualities that intrigue us and inspire us to make mobiles. Not only do we create a design that pleases us in all its phases, we make visible that which is invisible—the air currents come alive; their direction can be seen, and their tempo changes can be watched as the mobile moves with quiet grace or dances round and round.

Mobiles should be made so that the various sections will not touch, no matter how they move. And the real trick of making a mobile is in the balancing. Always start at the bottom and work toward the top, balancing each section as you go along. The "bottom" of the mobile is the lowest crossarm or supporting piece, not necessarily the shape that hangs down the lowest. This is shown in the photograph of the bell mobile.

Mobiles can be made of many kinds of material. Try a shell mobile, or one made of tiny baskets of flowers. If rock hunting is one of your hobbies, fasten threads to your most colorful stones and balance them in a mobile. The possibilities are endless. Here are just a few to start you off.

BELL MOBILE

For this mobile you will need six bells, three pieces of 16-gauge wire (either copper, which is very pliable and easy to use, or regular iron wire), black thread, and glue. The wires are 3 inches, 5 inches, and 7 inches long.

The bells are made of half circles of metallic foil stapled to form cones. Black thread is attached inside the bell with a touch of glue.

With long-nosed pliers, make an "eye," turning it under, at each end of the three pieces of wire—don't quite close the eyes. Attach a bell by its thread to each end of the shortest wire, knotting the thread and securing it and smoothing it with a touch of glue. With the pliers, close the wire eye as tight as you can.

I always find the balance point of each section of a mobile by placing the wire across my finger, as shown in the photograph. Because the bells are the same size, the balance point of this bottom section of the mobile should be the center of the wire. At the balance point, make a loop in the wire, turning it upward. I like to use my hands for this, but you may find it easier to use pliers.

After making the loop at the balance point, carefully straighten out the cross-arm so that it runs in a slight curve from one bell to the other, keeping both eyes and the balance-point loop parallel.

Run a thread through the loop at the balance point, and hold up the bottom section of your mobile to make sure it is properly balanced. The loop can be moved one way or the other with pliers to correct balance.

Attach the thread in loop of balance point to one end of the middle-sized piece of wire, knotting and gluing it securely. Leave about an inch of thread between the two wires. Tighten the eye.

Attach three bells to one thread—a bit of glue will hold them—and hang the cluster to the other end of the second piece of wire. Knot the thread, secure with glue, and tighten the eye.

Then find the balance point of the two sections of your mobile by suspending across your finger. At the balance point turn a loop upward, attach thread, hold up to see that it is in balance, and attach to one end of the longest piece of wire. Attach the last bell to the other end of the top wire, find balance point, turn a loop, attach a thread —and your mobile is completed.

ANGEL MOBILE

A three-piece mobile is one of the simplest to make. These three angels float freely in space, each one seemingly independent of the others and yet maintaining a relationship to the others.

Besides the three angels, you will need two 8-inch pieces of 16-gauge wire, black thread, and glue. For instructions on making the angels, see the chapter on decorations that hang.

Make "eyes" in each end of the two pieces of wire, as for the bell mobile. Attach an angel to each end of one wire, using a shorter thread for one so that it will hang higher than the other. Because the angels are the same size, the balance point of this bottom section should be in the middle of the wire crossarm. Make a loop at the balance point, attach a thread, and then fasten the thread to one end of the second piece of wire. Attach the third angel to the other end of the second wire, and place crossarm across your finger to find the balance point of the entire mobile. Turn a loop at that point and run a thread through it and suspend the mobile.

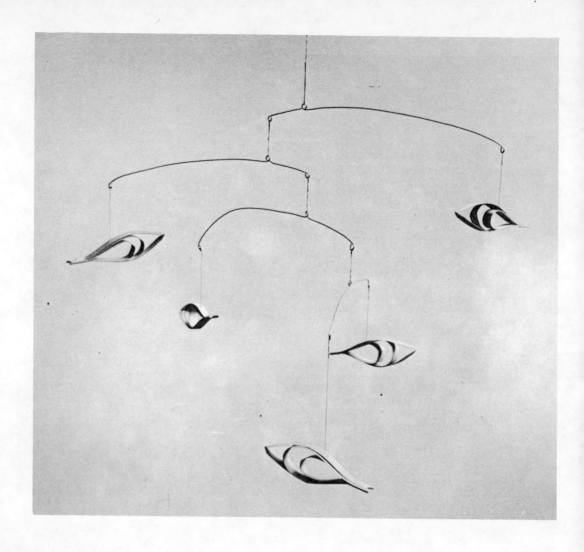

BIRD MOBILE

Four feathered friends fly by, as the fifth comes circling back. Birds are excellent for mobiles as the air is their natural element and they seem right at home. And five is a good number—it gives an asymmetrical configuration.

This mobile takes four pieces of wire, the bottom one 7 inches long. Each succeeding wire is ½ inch longer than the one below it—so that you need wires 7, 7½, 8, and 8½ inches long.

Proceed exactly as with the angel mobile, adding two more wires and two more birds. For instructions on making the birds, see the chapter on decorations that hang.

This mobile moves easily with the slightest air current because the wings provide fairly large surfaces to catch the air. Use two colors, perhaps blue for the bodies and yellow for the wings of three of the birds and reverse the colors for two, giving them yellow bodies and blue wings.

Your birds will never stop flying!

FISH MOBILE

The fish mobile is designed exactly like the bird mobile. But the fish move more deliberately because they have no flat surfaces to catch the air. It almost seems as though they were swimming.

These fish are 4 inches long. Each one is made of three strips of construction paper—an 8-inch strip, a 6-inch strip, and a 5-inch strip, each ¾ inch wide. The strips are stapled together, one inside the other, notched for the tail, pointed for the nose. Each fish is suspended by a thread. (See chapter on decorations that hang.)

Use two colors (mine are blue and green) and copper wire for this one. It has more delicacy than the iron wire and somehow the fish seem to require the coppery sheen.

RINGS FROM OUTER SPACE

Mobile greeting cards are fun to make for your special friends. Here a series of circles twirl one within the other, like something from outer space.

Start with a Circle

On a sheet of bright red construction paper, draw nine circles, one outside the next, graduated in size. Use the same central point and these diameters: 1 inch, 1½ inches; 2½ inches; 3 inches; 4 inches; 4½ inches; 5½ inches; 6 inches; and finally, for the largest circle, use a diameter of 7 inches. (If you use a compass and if you set your compass with a ruler, use *half* these measure-ments, because you will be measuring the *radius*.)

After all nine circles are drawn, cut on every line. You will end up with four rings, each ½ inch wide, and a center-piece an inch across. (You will also, of course, have four rings, each ¼ inch wide, but discard these.)

Arrange the rings within each other, placing the center circle exactly in the middle. Put a dab of glue along one ra-dius, starting at the center point and going to the outer edge. Along this line

of glue, place a thread of matching color, leaving plenty of thread with which to hang the mobile. It will dry in a moment. Write your holiday greeting on the center circle.

STYLIZED CHRISTMAS TREE

A mobile Christmas card in the shape of a stylized tree is made from a triangle of green construction paper.

Start with a Triangle

Cut a triangle 7 inches by 7 inches by 6 inches, with the shortest side forming the base of the tree. Inside this triangle, draw another 5½ inches by 5½ inches by 4½ inches, and then another one 5 inches by 5 inches by 4 inches; then one 3½ inches by 3½ inches by 2¼ inches; and finally a triangle 2¾ inches by 2¾ inches by 2¼ inches. Cut on all lines and you will have three "trees" to suspend, one within the other. The center triangle is solid.

Arrange the triangles carefully, with the center one exactly in the middle. From the top point of the center triangle, run a matching thread with a bit of glue on it up through the points of the

other two triangles, leaving a long piece to hang the mobile by.

As the mobile moves, the "tree" becomes three-dimensional. Write a Christmas message on the center triangle—and mail the mobile.

CHRISTMAS-TREE MOBILE

Here's another mobile that can be used for a greeting card.

Start with a Triangle

Out of green construction paper, cut a triangle 6 inches by 6 inches by 8 inches, with the 8 inches forming the base. This will give you a short and squatty triangle. Starting at the bottom, cut it into strips ¾ inch wide. The point at the top will be 1½ inches deep. Cut a tapered piece for the pot the tree appears to be standing in—a piece about 1½ inches high, 2 inches across the top, and 1¼ across the bottom.

Arrange the pieces carefully on a newspaper, placing the strips about ½ inch apart. Run a thread from the bottom to the top, through the center of each piece, and fasten with glue. Be very sure your thread is in the exact center of each piece or your tree mobile

will be lopsided. Leave plenty of thread at top to use for hanging the mobile.

Cut matching triangles, if you like, or triangles of different colors, and run the thread between them. I like to alternate the colors—one red strip, then one green, then another red one.

STANDING MOBILE

This Christmas-ball mobile, 12 inches high, makes a charming conversation piece for your coffee table.

Proceed step by step from the bottom to the top. Use tiny Christmas balls, four that measure ½ inch in diameter and five measuring 1 inch in diameter. Use one color or perhaps two—no more. Mine is gold and green.

No thread is used for this mobile, except at the top, so that it moves as a unit. The balls are attached to the wire crossbars by their wire loops.

You will need eight pieces of 18-gauge wire: two 2½-inch pieces, four 3-inch pieces, and two 4-inch pieces.

Starting at the bottom, attach ½-inch balls to each end of a 2½-inch piece of

140

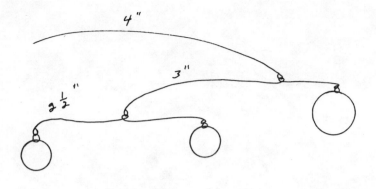

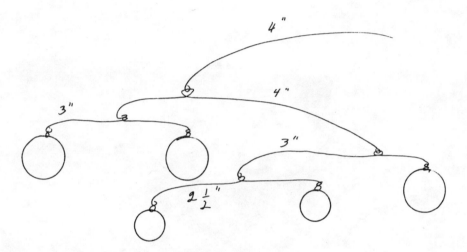

wire (first making an "eye" at the ends of the wires with long-nosed pliers). Turn a loop at the balance point (which will be the center, as the balls are the same size), and to this loop attach one end of a 3-inch piece of wire. At the other end attach a 1-inch ball. Find the balance point, turn a loop, and attach a 4-inch piece of wire. Your mobile now looks like the first sketch.

Next, attach 1-inch balls to each end of a 3-inch wire, turn a loop at the balance point (the center this time), and attach this unit to the other end of the 4-inch wire. Turn a loop at the balance

point, and to this loop attach one end of a 4-inch wire. Your mobile now looks like the second sketch.

To the other end of this 4-inch wire, attach a unit of 1-inch balls on a 3-inch wire. Again find a balance point.

You now have two wires and two balls left to use. Attach one end of the 3-inch wire remaining to the balance-point loop of the preceding 4-inch piece, and to the other end attach a unit of 1-inch balls on the remaining 2½-inch wire—this unit is just like the one you started with.

Find the balance point of the very

top crossbar, turn a loop, and suspend your mobile by a small loop of thread. Hang on a table standard, leaving 1½ inches between the top of the mobile and the hook of the standard.

STANDARD FOR THE TABLE MOBILE

The standard for the standing mobile has a wooden base, 3½ inches by 4½ inches, cut from ½-inch plywood and painted black. The bracket is made of 10-gauge brass wire (this is 1/16 inch thick) curved in a semicircle. A loop at the top holds the mobile. The bottom ¼ inch of the wire is bent at a right angle and fitted into a 1/16-inch hole drilled in the base about 1 inch in from the shorter edge.

When Christmas is over and your mobile is packed away for another season,

use the standard for another mobile—perhaps an abstract one of your own design. Or make one of a spade, a heart, a diamond, and a club, and use it for your next bridge party.

PEAR-TREE MOBILE

The pear-tree mobile, with its partridge perched on the center wire, is made of very thin copper sheeting. The bird is made of metallic foil.

The design of the mobile is more complex, but it is made in the same way as the simpler ones—starting at the bottom, each section is balanced as one proceeds toward the top. Use 18-gauge wire, and try your own design. Coat the "pears" and the wires with clear lacquer (or clear nail polish) to prevent tarnishing.

CHRISTMAS FANTASIA

Gold and silver metallic-foil fringe was used for a sort of mobile fantasia.

Cut small pieces of metallic-foil fringe about 1 inch long, reverse one piece, and weave the fringe together, as shown in photograph. Place a piece of black thread between the two pieces and fasten with glue. This makes the top of the three forms of the mobile, a sort of cap by which to suspend the form.

The bottom part of the bell forms (center and left in photograph) are made of 3-inch sections of fringe woven together and glued inside the "cap."

For the feathery form at the right (top), glue 3-inch woven pieces inside the cap as with the bell shapes. Then add at each side 1-inch pieces woven together, placing them at right angles to the cap.

Attach the threads to wire crossbars 6 inches long, balancing each section as you go along—from the bottom to the top. Make the threads of different lengths so each shape will hang at a different level—about 2 inches apart.

The foil catches the light as it catches the air, so that it glitters as it moves.

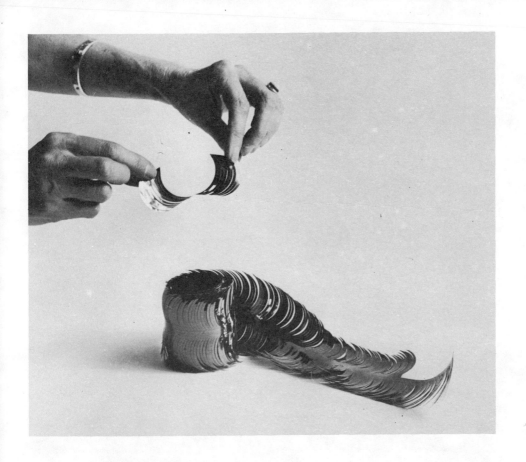

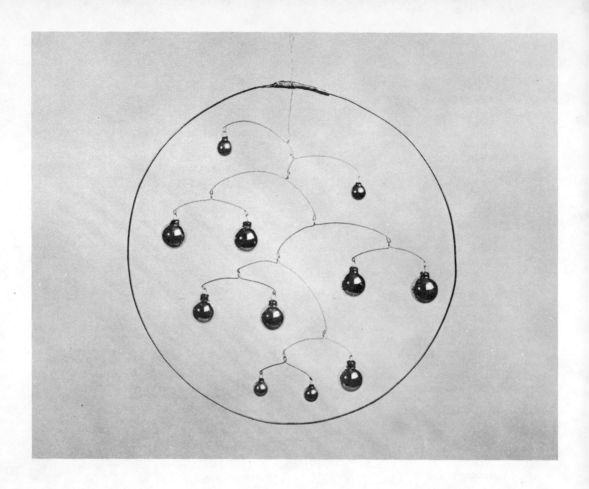

THE GOLDEN CIRCLE

Christmas-tree balls in a circle of gold —this mobile hangs parallel with the wall and is 12 inches in diameter.

You will need four Christmas-tree balls ½ inch in diameter and seven balls 1 inch in diameter. Use one color or perhaps two, but no more.

Cut ten pieces of 16-gauge wire in these sizes: two 3-inch pieces, five 4-inch pieces, and three 6-inch pieces. Cover each wire with gold paint.

Start at the bottom and balance each section as you go along. No thread is used, the balls being attached by their wire loops. (See drawings.)

1. Attach ½-inch balls to each end of a 3-inch wire (using long-nosed pliers to make a loop at each end of the wire). Turn a loop at the balance point. (See photograph for the bell mobile.) This time the balance point will be in the center of the arm because the balls are the same size. With pliers, give the loop a quarter turn so that it sits at right angles to the wire crossarm, as shown in sketch. (Every balance-point loop in this mobile is turned at right angles to the wire arm. This keeps the mobile in one plane.)

2. To this balance-point loop, attach one end of a 4-inch wire (again using

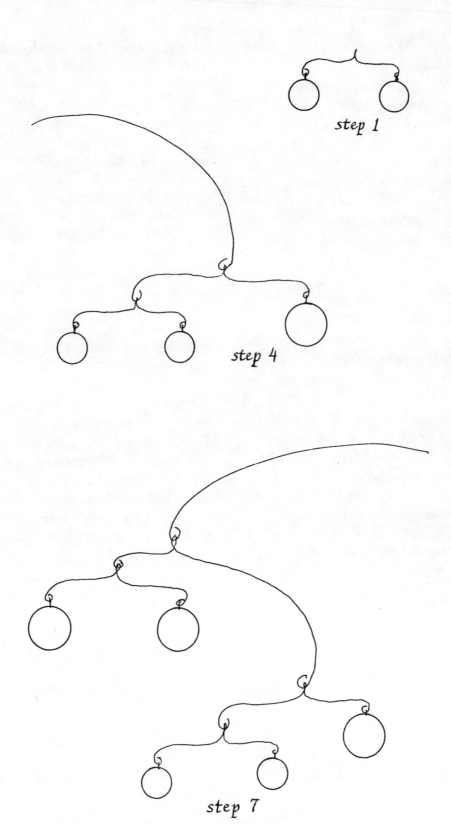

step 1

step 4

step 7

pliers). To the other end of the 4-inch wire, attach a 1-inch ball.

3. Find the balance point, turn a loop, and give the loop a quarter turn.

4. To this loop, attach a 6-inch wire, pointing it in the opposite direction. (See sketch.)

5. To each end of a 4-inch wire, attach a 1-inch ball. Turn a loop at the balance point (the center) and give the loop a quarter turn. Attach this unit to the other end of the 6-inch wire in step number 4.

6. Find the balance point, turn a loop, and give it a quarter turn.

7. To this loop, attach a 6-inch wire, again in the opposite direction.

8. To each end of a 4-inch wire, attach a 1-inch ball. Turn loop at balance point, giving loop a quarter turn. Attach unit to 6-inch wire in step number 7.

9. Find the balance point, turn a loop, and give it a quarter turn.

10. To this loop, attach the last 6-inch wire, in the opposite direction.

11. To each end of a 4-inch wire, attach a 1-inch ball. Turn loop at balance point (the center) and give loop a quarter turn. Attach this unit to end of 6-inch wire in step number 10.

12. Find the balance point, turn a loop, and give it a quarter turn.

13. To this loop, attach the last 4-inch wire, in the opposite direction.

14. To the other end of the 4-inch wire, attach a ½-inch ball.

15. Find the balance point, turn a loop, and give it a quarter turn.

16. To this loop, attach in opposite direction the *last* wire (3-inch), and attach a ½-inch ball to the other end.

17. Find balance point. Put a very fine wire through the balance-point loop— and this time don't bother with the quarter turn.

For the golden circle you will need a piece of 10-gauge wire 41 inches long. Form a circle, overlapping ends of wire and securing with masking tape. Paint the circle gold. This will give you a circle 12 inches in diameter.

Suspend the mobile inside the circle. It should just about fill the space. Hang from a wall bracket.

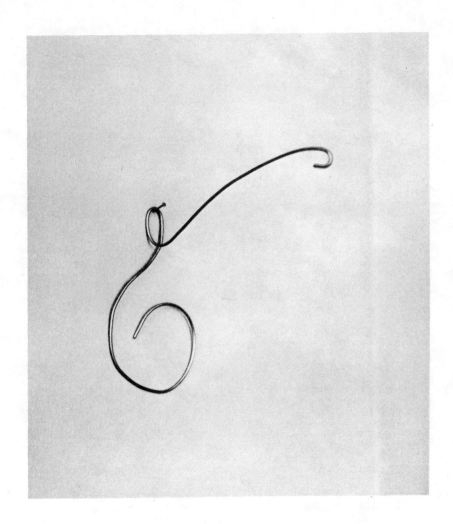

WALL BRACKET

The wall bracket is made of a piece of 10-gauge wire 30 inches long. With pliers, shape the wire to form a sort of G-clef, as shown in photograph. Make the arm about 10 inches long. The G-clef acts as a brace against the wall for the arm. Paint it gold or silver and hang from a hook.

The bracket is useful for mobiles, candle chandeliers, and other hanging decorations.

☆

CHAPTER IX

WHAT TO DO WITH YOUR CHRISTMAS CARDS

What do you do with your Christmas cards? You open them joyfully, admire them extravagantly, display them prominently—and then what do you do with them? When Christmas is over and the decorations come down, do you look at the cards once more and then ruefully relegate them to the rubbish pile? Don't do it!

Your Christmas cards are treasures of more than passing fancy. Tuck them away—and remember where you put them! Next season when the snows are swirling around and Christmas is on the way, get out the scissors, ruler, and paste pot and your carefully saved treasures—last year's Christmas cards. You'll find dozens of things to do with them. Here are just a few.

CUTOUT PLACE CARDS

Place cards for your family dinner can be made of Christmas-card cutouts. Make them in series—trees, candles, Madonnas. For the children's table use cutouts of Santas or angels. Here is a forest of trees for a party of six.

Cut out the figures with embroidery scissors. The trick is to silhouette them completely, taking out every bit of background. For the base, use colored construction paper or plain white bond, about 2 inches by 4 inches, depending on the size of the cutouts. A strip of the same paper, ¼ inch wide, is pasted to one edge of the base and then to the figure, as shown in the sketch. Paste the shaded area. Let the figure stand off-center, leaving space on the base for the dinner guest's name.

Lift the figure gently up and back, and it will stand on the base. To fold flat, tuck the base up behind the figure.

Make place cards of Madonnas, both modern and traditional. The Three Wise Men make excellent cutouts too.

THREE WISE MEN

These Wise Men stand about 6 inches tall and are richly colored and bright with gold. Larger cutouts such as these can be used to trim a mantel or a buffet table. Stand them on bases like the place cards.

Be sure to cut out all the background, even around the tassels on the Wise Men's caps and between their bodies, as you can see in the Wise Men on the

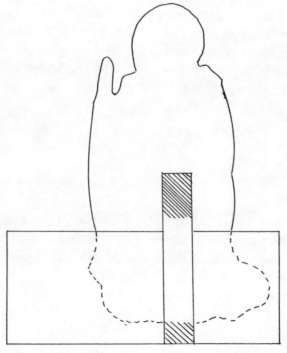

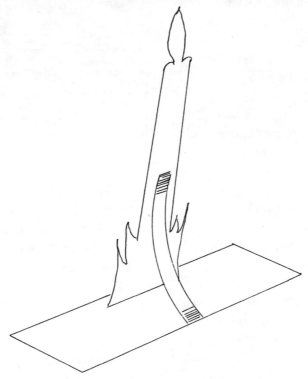

153

right of the photograph, and around the points of the crowns of those at the left.

ADVENT CALENDAR

An Advent calendar for your door—an inside door, as it won't withstand the weather—is made with Christmas cards. It's fascinating to do, and when it's finished it will add to the air of expectancy that prevails all during December.

Use brightly colored construction paper—mine is a rosy-red—6 inches wide and 32 inches long. This means that you will have to use two pieces, each 6 inches by 16 inches, and join them at the back with cellophane tape, covering the joint on the front with garlands of holly cut from Christmas cards.

First, measure and mark the twenty-four windows and doors (one for each day of December, from the first to Christmas Eve). I made windows above the center garland and doors below it, all of them 1 inch wide except the top three.

The window at the top is 1 inch high and 2 inches wide. The two under it are 1 inch by 1½ inches. Then the next three rows of windows are 1 inch by 1 inch each. The windows just above the holly garland are 1 inch by 1½ inches.

The doors in the first row under the garland are 2 inches high, the others 2½ inches high.

When the doors and windows are all drawn with pencil, place the calendar on a board or a heavy cardboard and cut—carefully—with a razor blade across the top and bottom, and down through the middle of each window and door.

Cut against a ruler edge. Bend back the shutters and doors.

Paste a strip of shelf paper on the back of the calendar, putting paste around the edges only.

Then comes the search for tiny figures to fill each door and window! Cut out little angels, kittens, and candles, and paste them inside the shutters onto the shelf paper underneath.

On the outside of the shutters and doors paste strips of patterns in gold, or

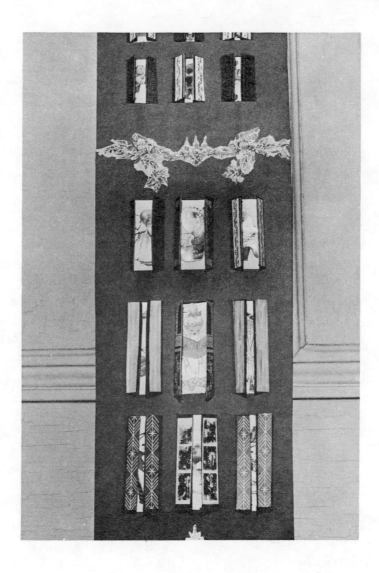

stained-glass strips from church scenes, matching and mixing as you like. You may even be lucky and find a window in your cards like the one in the center of the bottom row on mine.

The house must have a roof, of course —you'll find one somewhere among your cards. And the star of Bethlehem shines in the sky. At the bottom is the Christmas tree, set up for Christmas Eve.

Taper the top and round off the bottom, and finish off the calendar with a garland of holly like the one in the center. Open a window a day and watch the weeks go by, until it's time for Christmas.

The close-up of the Advent calendar shows the tiny figures inside the little doors—an angel singing, a little child with a muff sitting on a sled—and the patterns on the shutters. Formal Christmas cards are often edged with designs in gold and silver that can be used for this purpose.

CHILDREN'S GAME OF CUTOUTS

Here's a game for the children's party. Give each child half a dozen cutouts already pasted to their bases. Mix them up so that each child has a variety of forms.

Give them ten minutes to set up their characters. The prize goes to the child who creates the best scene.

If you have enough cards and scissors and paste pots, and plenty of time, let the children start at the beginning, cutting out the figures and pasting them to their bases. Again, the prize goes to the best scene or the scene that tells the best story: The galloping knight is headed for the old-fashioned lady holding Christmas candy in her bowl, while the rooster stands watching and the poodle goes on tying a knot on his Christmas package.

Many candles light the manuscript the old monk is working on.

The dog with the bell on his tail offers a Christmas branch to a curious rooster.

The little Japanese lady stands and watches the Santa, the choir boy, and the snowman singing Christmas carols.

SHADOW BOXES FOR YOUR TREASURES

One of the nicest—and simplest—ways to display your small figurines and trinkets is in shadow boxes. And one of the easiest kinds to make is the Christmas-card shadow box.

Select a scene from among your cards of last year, one that will enhance your figurine or animal or miniature. It might be a street scene for a doll, as shown here, a red barn for a tiny cow or rooster, a snowy road for the desert-loving camel and his master, or a forest for your ceramic tree.

Find a box to fit the card, cover it with construction paper of a color that will go with your scene, and paste the card inside the box. If it doesn't quite fit, make a sort of frame around the card of the construction paper used to cover the box.

Form a frame for the box, either one cut from a Christmas card or an edging made of gold braid or lace. Glue the "frame" to the shadow box and stand the box on the mantel or table, or fasten it to a wall.

If you have a card that especially appeals to you but no treasure to put in it, cut a figure from another card, mount it on a base and stand the cutout in the shadow box to make it three-dimensional.

[35] A non-melting snowman can set the mood for your holiday decorations. His hat is made of paper, his scarf of satin ribbon. See Chapter VII.

[36] Old-fashioned dolls bring a touch of nostalgia to the Christmas scene. Heads are made of walnuts and blown-out eggs. Chapter I.

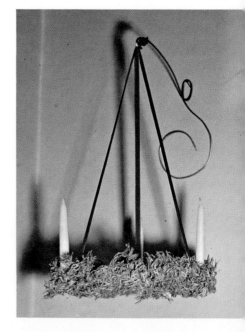

[37] A chandelier of princess pine and candles is suspended over the party table. For the details, see Chapter V.

[38] Dolls dressed in gingham stand among the Christmas packages under the tree. For complete instructions, see Chapter I.

[39] An Eastern cathedral, painted in bright colors and trimmed with towers of construction paper, protects the Christ Child and crib cut from a Christmas card. See Chapter VII.

[40] Branches trimmed with little red hearts from Sweden are fastened in a red container. For details, see Chapter VII.

[41] Tissue-paper ball tops the Christmas tree or hangs in the hallway. Complete instructions are given in Chapter VI.

161

[42] Christmas packages with intriguing decorations and in all colors are achieved with cutouts from last year's Christmas cards. See Chapter IX.

[44] Posters of Christmas scenes are made on construction paper with cutouts. See Chapter IX for complete instructions.

[43] Lucia, the symbol of the season of light, carries a crown of candles in her hair. For instructions, see Chapter V.

SHELF-PAPER POSTER

In many parts of the world it is the custom to decorate the walls with colorful Christmas posters. In Scandinavia, particularly in the kitchen, bright posters are hung on the walls.

Cutouts from Christmas cards make marvelous posters. A roll of shelf paper, a pile of Christmas cards, scissors, and paste—and you won't hear a sound out of the children for the whole of a stormy day!

This one was made on a strip of white shelf paper, about 40 inches long. Part of the fun is choosing colors that go well together, and again the trick is to silhouette the figures completely. All of the candles across the bottom of the poster came from the same card.

The close-up of the shelf-paper poster shows how the cutouts can be grouped to tell stories. The candles are used as a device to separate one part of the tale from the next.

CONSTRUCTION-PAPER POSTER

Bright blue construction paper 18 inches long and 9½ inches wide was used for the poster of the carolers. Smaller posters such as this one need only one main idea. It sometimes takes quite a search through the cards to find the right cutouts.

MAKE FRAMES OF YOUR
CHRISTMAS CARDS

Many Christmas cards have scenes that are framed in gold or brightly colored borders. These can be used to frame your family photographs, and they are not only effective but will stand on their own.

Just cut out the scene, leaving the frame of the card intact, and slip your photograph into the open space. If the photograph is too large, trim it until it fits, and secure it in the frame with a touch of white glue. If the photograph is too small, give it an extra border of gold paper to fill the space between print and frame.

Stand the framed family portraits on a table or mantel—they will be quite well protected in their Christmas-card borders.

CHRISTMAS-CARD MOBILES

Mobiles of Christmas cards carry an abundance of holiday greetings. They are intriguing to make and not as simple as they seem to be.

In the first place, you must choose cards that go well together—colors and subjects should harmonize.

In the second place, each card must have one of a matching size to back it. If you can't find just the right card for this, use a piece of colored paper or Christmas wrapping paper that has an interesting design.

You must also have variation in shapes and sizes for your mobile. The pieces at top and bottom give it form. A small sleigh bell at the bottom is a fine finishing touch—but if you want to mail your mobile for a Christmas greeting, leave off the bell.

When you have chosen your cards, and the sequence in which you want them to hang, place them on a table in their proper order, with their *wrong* sides facing up. Run a black thread down the entire length of the mobile, through the center of each card. If thread is not exactly in the center of each card, the mobile will not hang properly. Add a few dabs of glue to the thread where it touches the cards, and

place the matching cards on top of the thread, *right* side up. Leave enough thread at the top to make a loop for hanging.

If you have received an unusual card from a good friend, feature it in a mobile and send it back the following year!

CHILDREN'S PLACE CARDS

Cutouts of children are always appealing. These can be made into simple place cards that are especially good for the children's table.

Choose figures of about the same size —3 to 4 inches tall. For the base, use plain white cards 4 inches square, or use 4-inch squares of colored construc-

tion paper. Fold the square in half and paste the figure to the folded card, slightly off-center so that there will be room for the name. These place cards make colorful and attractive additions to the party table.

Make them in sets for Christmas gifts. As long as the figures are not taller than the *unfolded* cards, they will pack nicely in an envelope.

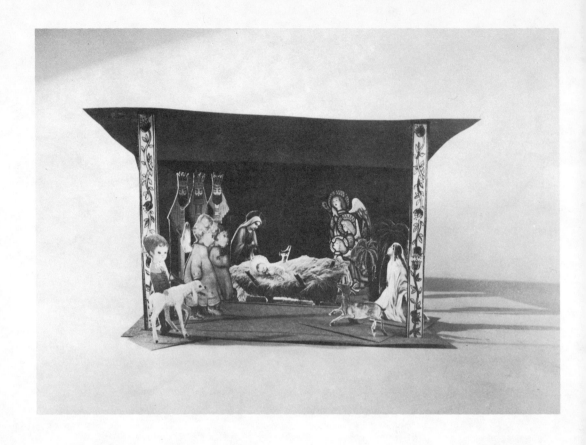

CHRISTMAS-CARD CRÈCHE

The Christmas-card crèche can be made in any size you like, according to the size of your figures. I made mine of a piece of Bristol board 18 inches long and 12 inches wide. I shaped the strip, as shown in the accompanying sketch, so that it tapered from 12 inches (across the front of the roof) to 8 inches (at the bottom of the back wall) and then widened again to 10 inches for the front edge of the floor. Fold along dotted lines. The floor is 7 inches from front to back; then the cardboard is bent up to form the back wall, which is 4½ inches high. Another bend brings the roof forward for 6½ inches.

The pillars that support the roof are strips of cardboard ½ inch wide and 8 inches long. These are glued in place inside the roof. Then, instead of gluing the other ends of the pillars to the floor, I made ½-inch slits at the places where the pillars should stand, bent the last ½ inch of the pillars, and slipped them through the slits. This makes it possible to fold the crèche flat and store it away for another year.

The pillars are decorated with designs cut from a Christmas card. The figures in the crèche are Christmas-card cutouts fastened to bases just as the place cards are. The side view of the crèche shows how the figures are grouped, some at the back and some in front, to create the Nativity scene.

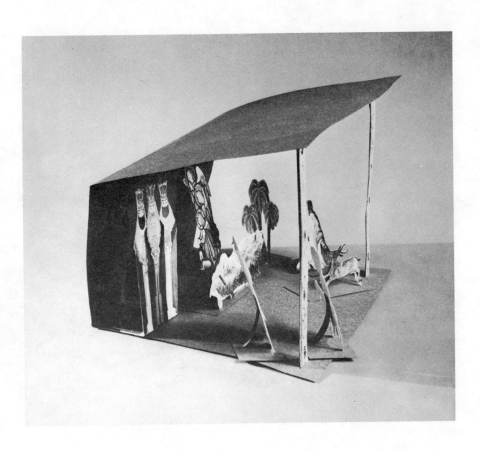

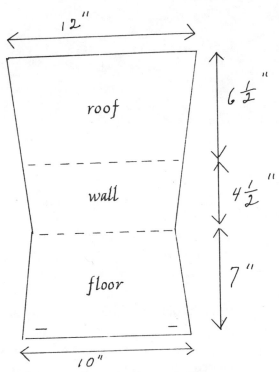

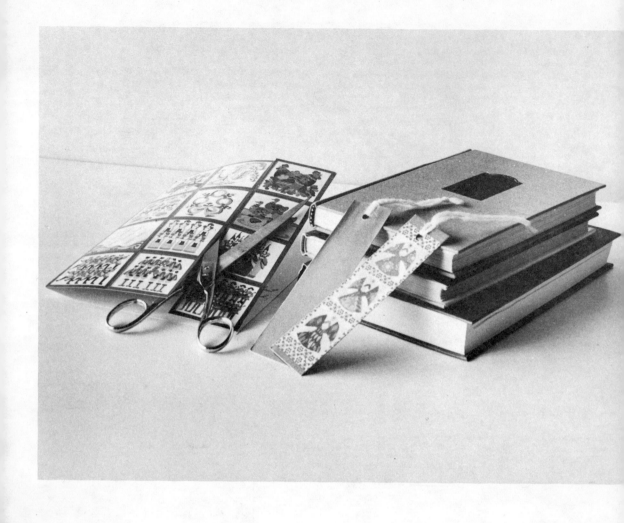

CHRISTMAS BOOKMARKS

Quick, easy, and very colorful, these bookmarks can be fashioned from last year's Christmas cards. Be sure to choose cards with a pattern that can be cut into inch-wide strips.

Glue gold paper, also cut from an old Christmas card, to the back of the bookmark. Punch a hole near one end and slip a piece of gold cord or colored yarn through. If you don't have a punch, make a hole with the point of your manicure scissors and cut a small, round hole. Tie a knot in the ends so the bookmark can be hung on the Christmas tree. Or place them on the Christmas dinner table as favors, one for each guest—and you can also use them as colorful and useful Christmas cards for your very special friends.

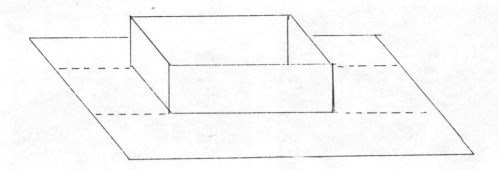

CHRISTMAS WRAPPINGS

All those pretty packages piled high around the Christmas tree are trimmed with colors carefully chosen and ribbons tied just *so*. Finally, it is time for the family to gather round the tree, and the annual package-opening ceremony begins. Moments later the pretty packages have vanished. Piles of crumpled paper and strands of torn-up bows fill the floor.

You can keep your package pretty and open it too if you wrap the box and its cover separately. Cut a piece of paper large enough to cover the bottom part of the box and to go down ½ inch inside it. Place box in the center of the paper, snip paper to each corner of the box (see sketch), and fasten with glue. Then put wrapping paper on the cover in the same fashion, fastening paper ½ inch up inside the cover.

Decorate the cover and tie up the box—or use cellophane tape to keep the cover on. When the time comes to open the package, snip ribbon or tape and keep your decorations intact.

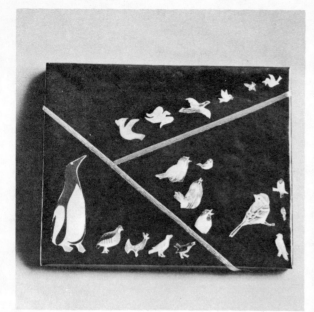

DECORATE WITH CUTOUTS

Christmas-card cutouts can add to the fun of decorating your packages. Choose cutouts to suit the gift or the one to whom it goes. For instance, if the package contains a book, cut out all the candles you can find and create a design on the cover of the box to light the reader's way. Run ribbon across two corners and tie at the back of the package.

Birds that sit and birds that stand, birds flying and perching, singing and walking—collect them all to trim gifts for your friends who watch the birds.

Narrow strips of gold-colored sticky tape serve two purposes—they define the design and hold the cover on the box. Three snips of the scissors and the cover lifts off without destroying the design.

The long and narrow box seems to be made for three pink angels separated by gold cord and two simple bows. The box is wrapped in green foil.

The green and gold of the Madonna and the other figures in this religious scene are carried out in the gold wrapping and green satin ribbon.

A big package for a tiny tot is trimmed with a cageful of kiddies coming down the hill, to be met by Grandpa below.

Strips of gold-colored cellophane tape placed around the package separate the cutouts, forming the cage, and also keep the cover on. Snip the tape to open the box.

TRIPTYCH SCREEN

Screens, both large and small, are useful, decorative, colorful—and if you like, seasonal. Small ones can be made with scenes cut from last year's Christmas cards and a few pieces of cardboard, gold paper, and gold cord.

First, choose three cards of similar subjects—I chose Madonnas for mine, but you might prefer winter scenes or snowmen or Santas, or whatever—and keep enough of the background to fill your panels.

Next, cut out three panels of heavy cardboard, or corrugated cardboard, of a size that will accommodate your cutouts. Round off the tops. My panels are

about 5 by 7 inches. Trim the cutouts to match the panels exactly.

Hinge the cardboard panels together with strapping tape—a cellophane tape that has threads running through it for strength.

Glue the cutouts to one side and the gold paper (also cut from Christmas cards) to the other side of each panel, and trim all edges with gold cord. Use white glue to fasten it.

If you have rounded the tops of your panels as I have (see photograph), run the gold cord down between each cutout, along the line of the hinge.

The screen will decorate your mantel, hide your telephone, or form a background for a buffet-table centerpiece.

Quick and Easy Variation

For a simple variation, cut a three-paneled screen out of red poster board, folding the sections into three equal divisions. (See picture at left.)

If the poster board cracks when it is folded, showing the white board inside, touch up the cracked spots with a red felt pen.

Glue a Christmas tree cut from last year's Christmas cards (as I have) to each panel, and trim each section with gold cord. Such a screen is easy to make and it is colorful as well, and you will find it useful in your Christmas decorations.

☆

CHAPTER X

MAKE YOUR OWN CHRISTMAS CARDS

Part of the fun of getting ready for Christmas is making your own Christmas cards—perhaps not all of them, but a few special ones for a few special friends.

There are many ways to make cards, and many different kinds of materials to use. Here are a few suggestions to start you off.

Plain cards and matching envelopes, in several different colors—red, green, medium blue, gray, gold, white—are available in all art-supply shops. These are fine as the foundations for your own designs.

LACE CARDS

Tree shapes are traditional and are easy to make. They are particularly effective made with lace. Cut strips in graduated lengths, from about 1 inch for the top to 4 inches for the bottom. Give the tree a bow at the top and a base at the bottom. Attach the lace with Pritt Glue Stick—it will not show and will not smear your card.

Lace trees can also be made of paper-lace doilies—either white or gold or silver paper. Use the edges of the doily, and form the tree with graduated strips.

For a card with candles trimmed with lace (see photograph), cut narrow strips of gold or colored foil and edge them with lace. Cut circles of gold paper for the halo around the flame, and make the flame of dark-colored paper centered with a snip of gold paper shaped like the center of the flame. Attach with Pritt Glue Stick.

If you want to have an angel on your card, use lace 2 inches wide. Cut the wings (experiment with newspaper first, until you get a shape for a pattern that you like), and then make the body of the full width of the lace, gathering it at the waist as you glue it to the card. Cut an oval of gold paper for the face, and give the angel a lace crown.

FELT CARDS

Felt in bright colors makes fine designs for cards. For a farm scene, cut barns and silo of pink felt, give them white roofs, and cut tiny doors of dark brown. Attach with Pritt Glue Stick.

For a church scene, cut the church out of white felt and glue it to a dark blue card. Give the church a blue roof

and fence off the churchyard with short pieces of white yarn.

Felt bells tied with ribbons are cut from green felt. Follow the bell pattern given, and cut the ribbons and the clappers of white felt. Mount the design on a card of contrasting color.

For the little tomte holding his Christmas tree, cut the cap and the triangular robe and his tree of red felt, glue to a white card, leaving the space for the face empty. Draw in eyes and nose with a felt pen. Add a white felt beard and a white felt topknot on his cap.

The possibilities are endless. Once you start, you will find many variations on the theme.

THREE-DIMENSIONAL CARDS

Three-dimensional cards are fun to make too. For the mobilelike Christmas tree with its swinging bell, start with a piece of green construction paper 10 inches long and 4 inches wide. Fold in half. Trace the tree shape given in the pattern here onto each side of the folded card, and cut out with a razor or an X-Acto knife. Cut two bells of gold paper and glue them together with a 3-inch piece of gold cord in between. Attach the bell to the folded card by pulling the cord up through a small hole in the center of the fold. Knot the cord so

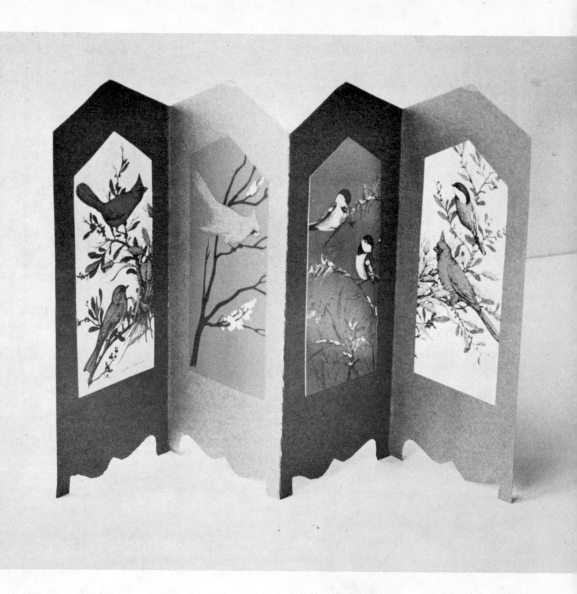

the bell will swing freely in the tree-shaped opening. Stand the card up, as shown in the photograph.

SCREEN

Another way to make a card is to start with a strip of colored paper 12 inches long and 7½ inches wide. Fold into four sections, making a screen with four panels. Cut the tops into points (or round them off) and cut the bottom of the sections to give them feet. (See photograph.)

Look through your last year's Christmas cards and find cutouts to paste onto your screen panels. Choose similar subjects—I found an assortment of birds—and write your Christmas message on the back of the screen.

GIFT CARDS

For a welcome present for a special friend, make a set of greeting cards that can be used anytime through the year. Start with the plain cards available in an art-supply shop, and decorate them with scenes that appeal to you from magazines. Choose colorful advertisements and illustrations, trim them to a size to fit your cards, and attach them with Pritt Glue Stick. Use a razor or X-Acto knife to cut your scenes, and cut against a ruler that has a steel edge.

This will produce a smooth, professional-looking edge.

STENCIL

For fun and fantasy, try using sections of a plastic berry basket as a stencil, and, with the help of colored felt pens, make up a fantastic collection of designs for Christmas. If you mix and match the openings, combine them and turn them up and down, you will discover all sorts of shapes and designs for very original Christmas cards.

☆

SOURCES FOR MATERIALS

Simple materials, easy to find, are the best ones to use for making decorations. Some materials, usually used once and then tossed away, can be turned into valuable treasures and decorations with just a little paint, gold cord, and bright cutouts—and a little imagination. These include tin cans, cardboards, plastic containers, boxes of various sorts and sizes. Before you throw packagings away, consider their possibilities.

Paper of all sorts and colors, in many different sizes, is available in dime stores, art-supply shops, and handcraft shops.

Construction paper comes in packages of fifty sheets in assorted colors, usually 12 inches by 18 inches.

Metallic foil is sold in packages of assorted colors, with silver on one side, in 9 by 12-inch sheets.

Tissue paper, in every color of the rainbow, is available in packages of fifty sheets, in stationery and art-supply shops.

Bristol board and poster board you'll find in your local art-supply shop in sheets of varying sizes, colors, and thick-nesses. These are usually sold by the sheet.

Crepe paper and Christmas wrapping paper are sold in every dime store.

Typing paper, or plain white bond, comes in small packages in dime and stationery stores.

Many different kinds of glue are available. Sobo and Elmer's (white glue) are easy to use on paper. Pritt Glue Stick, which comes in a tube like lipstick, works very well on paper and fabrics and does not smear. All glues are available in stationery shops, dime stores, and hardware stores.

Le Page's liquid solder works well with copper and aluminum. This is found in hardware shops.

Aluminum comes in 36-inch-square sheets at all hardware stores. One sheet is enough to make several sconces, several angels, and plenty of donkeys. Copper, too, is sold by the sheet in handcraft shops. It comes in various thicknesses, in sheets 15 inches square. I use 36-gauge for most of my decorations.

Glitter is packaged in small bottles—both gold and silver—and sometimes comes with a shaker top. It also comes in tubes already mixed with glue. Hardware shops, dime stores, and art-supply shops have it.

Oasis is sold in most florist shops. It is a foamlike material that comes in blocks and can be cut to fit your container. Soaked with water, it will keep flowers and greens fresh for many days.

Small bottles and cans of paint, as well as spray paints in all colors, are easy to find. Gold and silver too are available. You'll find these at hardware stores, hobby shops, and art-supply shops.

Felt is sold by the yard in all fabric departments. It is usually 54 or more inches wide. It is also available in hobby shops in 6-inch squares. Gold braid and cord are sold in notions departments.

Poly-fil, a fine filler made of polyester, comes in plastic bags in dime stores and department stores.

Cellophane tapes of all kinds—invisible, colored, and reinforced—are readily available in stationery, art-supply, and hardware stores.

Your hardware store will supply you with wire in whatever gauge you want, in small amounts or large. It comes on cards in 6-foot lengths—both copper and regular iron wire. Hardware stores also have spool wire, which is as fine as thread.

Your local hobby shop or dime store will supply you with plastic ribbon, embroidery hoops, and Styrofoam in all shapes and sizes.

Plaster of Paris is available in very small quantities in all hardware stores.

INDEX